# Ella's Story

## One Family's Journey to Discovering Miracles Do Happen

ANGELA McBRIDE

# ENDORSEMENTS

*"Ella's Story* is inspirational, showing how a young girl can endure, accept, and overcome incredible challenges truly one step at a time over many years. Her story also shows the power of blending medicine with faith and trust. This was on display not only in Ella and her family, but also included the doctors, surgeons, nurses, and staff who took part in Ella's journey firsthand."

—Chester Ho, M.D.
Ella's Pediatrician

"This is a great book to read because it is a real-life, journey-through-the-trenches, I-can-relate type of a story. You see, everyone has a story. It's what you do with that story that makes the difference! After you read it, my prayer is that you will find your own story to write (or tell)!"

—Pastor Randy Skidmore
Senior Pastor, Elston Family Church

"Angela McBride has written a book that takes us on a journey of her young family facing a rare and life-threatening diagnosis of their baby girl. This heartwarming journey of struggle, faith, community, and medical miracles is what we need, especially in 2020!"

—Deanna Wise-Frerichs
Educator

"Because of Jesus' bravery and love in giving His life for us, we, too, must be brave and share the testimony we have to give, and Angela has done just that. Not only are you reeled into reading more of Ella's journey to know how she fares, but also into the excitement of seeing God's handiwork in this family's struggle. Angela takes you into the hospital room with them and shares the raw feelings any parent would dread to have. Angela has written a captivating story of a beautiful and honest progression of faith, a mother's paradox of unfathomable love and unbearable fear, guidance for anyone going through a medical crisis, and proof we have a mighty God we can lean on through anything."

—Kristen Hamilton
**Women's Ministry Leader, Connection Point Church**

"You'll enjoy this honest reflection of a family's story and how you also can find strength in the hard press place in life. Our journeys may be different, but our needs and comforts are still the same. Connect with their sorrow, but also connect with their thankfulness and peace."

—Jessica Milsaps
**Owner and Lead Organizer, MILSAPS at HOME**

"*Ella's Story* details the remarkable medical journey of Ella McBride. Ella came into my care at a very young age when she presented with severe high blood pressure and was diagnosed with a rare syndrome called middle aortic syndrome where her aorta was significantly narrowed in the middle. Also, at the time of diagnosis, one of Ella's kidneys was significantly damaged with poor blood flow to the kidney. This book shares Ella's difficult journey from her initial diagnosis to multiple hospital stays, medications, and surgeries. Amazingly, Ella is now an outgoing, remarkable, and healthy young woman and has been able to discontinue all blood pressure medication, which I never would have expected. *Ella's Story* is one of heartache, healing, and hope."

—Sharon Phillips Andreoli, M.D.
Byron P. and Frances D. Hollett Emeritus Professor of Pediatrics

"'For I know the plans I have for you,' declares the LORD, 'plans to prosper you and not to harm you, plans to give you hope and a future.'"

Jeremiah 29:11 (NIV)

# Contents

# Acknowledgments

This book wouldn't have come to light if it weren't for God tugging at my heart to share our story. Even though I felt inadequate, thank You, Father, for working through me in the hope that our story will bring someone to You.

Thank you to our family and friends who helped us so immensely over the years, always ready at a moment's notice to be there for us. We couldn't have done it without you, and we are forever indebted to you.

Thank you to everyone who walked with us in the valley and prayerfully helped us out.

A huge thank you to all of the doctors and nurses who cared for Ella and who allow God to use you to save so many lives. A special thank you to Riley Hospital for Children for being such an awesome hospital.

Thank you to the people who created a wonderful avenue with the CaringBridge site that allowed us to update family and friends and to receive encouragement from them.

Thank you to Renee Fisher, Rebekah Benham, and Nelly Murariu for helping me with the book writing and publishing process and for helping to make this book as it was meant to be.

An incredibly huge thank you to my rock, biggest supporter, and partner in life, my husband Joe. Thank you for being you!

This book is dedicated to Joe, Noah, and Ella. May you seek the Lord in all you do. Thank you for encouraging me to complete this book and putting up with me these past several months. I love you!

"For God so loved the world, that he gave his only Son, that whoever believes in him should not perish but have eternal life."

(John 3:16, ESV)

# Foreword

by Alisha Cook, RN, BSN, CLC, CPST
Riley Hospital for Children at Indiana University Health

I was sitting in church one Sunday when my pastor said "Do you believe in miracles?......I mean, do you believe that God is still in the miracle-working business today like He was in the time when Jesus lived?" He defined a miracle as when God steps into what seems to be an impossible situation and intervenes with His amazing grace.

There are diagnoses that are always hard to hear about. The ones where the baby appears healthy, but the parents have been told that doctors haven't quite figured out the next steps. The ones where you know, as a nurse, just how sick they are, but mom and dad don't fully understand because they were given the shock of their lives just days ago. And then there are the ones that even you, as a nurse who devotes her life to taking care of sick babies, don't understand because this baby is sick with something so rare that you doubt your own abilities to care for them. And you are beyond terrified. This was me. This was them. I was that nurse tasked to care for sweet, sweet baby Ella.

Her pigtails were the first thing that caught my eye when I came into her hospital room...that and her name. I had never heard it before and instantly fell in love with it. I was a new nurse and newly pregnant and envisioned if I had a girl I would call her Ella. If it weren't for her pigtails and her amazing name, I would have first noticed her big blue eyes. They drew me to her, and I couldn't help but feel that she was beautiful and perfect all at once. I didn't fully grasp that this sweet girl was on the front end of a long, hard battle. Her family...well, they were also perfection. As a nurse, you straddle this line of balance between keeping your patients at arm's length and creating incredible connections with them. Ella's family was easy to love and one that I easily connected with.

I met her mama first and remember knowing that she was a woman of faith from our first conversations. I watched her journal, saturate the room with Christian music, and pray so hard for her daughter. It's heartbreaking to watch a mama pray in petition for her baby. We live in a fallen world, but we have a very loving God who, in scripture, says is always for our good. "'For I know the plans I have for you,' declares the LORD, 'plans to prosper you and not to harm you, plans to give you hope and a future'" (Jeremiah 29:11, NIV).

Very early on in my career, I started a routine doing a specific thing in certain situations. When hearing a code blue called, working on my own declining patient, with a family hearing a diagnosis of their baby, or handing a patient over to their family for the last time, I stop for a moment and I pray. I say a prayer of healing for that child and a prayer of peace for their loved ones. Every single time. Most of the time, I'm praying for a miracle. Did you know that in one study polling physicians on their stance of miracles, 74% say they believe miracles occur?

As a nurse, I admit that I have had thoughts teetering on who is doing the healing here—the doctors or God. Although I have faith, it is difficult to understand when the mortal ends and the divine begins. I learned that day in church that it isn't uncommon to have these thoughts. People struggle with it because they truly can't comprehend how it can be done. My pastor made things so clear during that sermon when he explained that when people make themselves available, God uses them in miracles. He is always there, orchestrating it all. Just like with Ella. He was there in the beginning and will continue orchestrating her complete story with utter perfection.

That is exactly what has happened from that first hospital room with that sweet girl. A mama petitioned, a nurse prayed, the staff used their gifts, my God healed, and a beautiful girl lived. A miracle was performed.

# PROLOGUE

## "My Story"

by Big Daddy Weave

"If I told you my story

You would hear Hope that wouldn't let go

And if I told you my story

You would hear Love that never gave up

And if I told you my story

You would hear Life, but it wasn't mine

If I should speak then let it be

Of the grace that is greater than all my sin

Of when justice was served and where mercy wins

Of the kindness of Jesus that draws me in

Oh to tell you my story is to tell of Him

If I told you my story

You would hear victory over the enemy

And if I told you my story

You would hear freedom that was won for me

And if I told you my story

You would hear Life overcome the grave"

The words from the Big Daddy Weave song "My Story" resonated so much with me. It was on New Year's Day a few years back when I first heard this song being played at church. My eyes started to tear up as I watched the video of a man sliding a piece of paper into the roller of an old-fashioned typewriter and the scenes phasing to different people sitting at the typewriter pecking at the keys to write their stories. Everyone has a story, each different and uniquely created. I knew at that moment that God was speaking to me and confirming that it was time to focus on sharing our story with you all. It's not an easy story to share as it is so personal. And, I will admit, there is a lot of heartache, challenge, and doubt, but there is also hope, love, grace, and healing. I pray that, as you read, you will find hope in the power of prayer and know that God loves you as His child. I also pray that if you are struggling with a trial that you will seek help from others whom the Lord has placed in your path.

Our story began about eight years before Ella came along. Joe, my husband, and I met in college and were married less than a year after graduating. We suffered a miscarriage early on in our marriage, along with the typical ups and downs that you expect in those first few years. We lived in Illinois for about five years before moving back to our home state of Indiana, where we both worked for a well-known insurance company. Joe worked in the compliance department while I was in auto claims. We enjoyed the time with family, friends, Joe's love of golf and vacationing, but we longed to start a family of our own. In September of 2003, a bouncing baby boy, Noah, came along. Noah ended up being a scheduled c-section as the little guy was in there backward, trying to kick his way out instead of going head first. I think he was already showing what a strong-willed child he was going to be. Nonetheless, he was a healthy, blue-eyed boy.

Going from the workforce to a stay-at-home wife/mom was a big change, but we agreed that it was what we wanted for our family. Sure, it was going to take some sacrifices, but ones we were willing to make. I love that Joe suggested a more official title for me: Home and Family Specialist. It sounded more formal.

And just twenty-two months later, Ella Rose was born into our family. Another blue-eyed cutie-patootie. We were adjusting to being a family of four when just about a year later our world was turned dramatically and suddenly upside down. Buckle up as our roller coaster ride of a journey begins to unfold, starting with the first CaringBridge post we shared.

# OUR FIRST CARINGBRIDGE POST

Monday, July 31, 2006, 11:19 p.m.
Journal entry written by Angela

*Dear All, Sorry to have to send this in an email instead of calling right now, but I am sure you will understand. I don't even know where to start. Ella has been admitted to the ICU here at St. Vincent Hospital in Indianapolis. She had developed a cold over the weekend and was having trouble breathing. Long story short, they have found that she has an enlarged heart and that the heart muscles are weak and not working properly. They are not sure of the cause yet and not sure of what long-term effects there may be. Dr. Ho consulted with the Pediatric Cardiologist here, and they decided this is the best place for her right now. The plan is to do a large variety of tests to hopefully pinpoint the problem. They do believe this is why she had not been gaining weight, so she has probably had a heart condition for a while. Her blood pressure is also so high for her age. That is another area they are looking into. At this point—prayer is what we need! The chaplain here has been so kind and so have all the doctors and nurses.*

*We have had so many medical terms thrown at us and with everything that poor little girl has been through today, I can't think straight. This is the last thing I ever thought we would have to deal with. Right now, the emergency room doctor is putting in a central line. (This will help if they need to give more than one medication at a time or draw blood). I thought I would take this time to let you all know and settle myself down a bit as well. I am pretty sure Mom is taking the rest of the week off and keeping Noah. The doctors have told us that we will be here at least a week. We're not sure what lies ahead, but we will certainly keep you posted when we can and please, please, pray for Ella.*

*Love, Angela and Joe*

So much had transpired in such a short amount of time that day. It was difficult to comprehend all that was going on and to know exactly what to share with everyone. No one but our closest family knew the true severity of the situation and how our world had just been turned upside down. It was something we would never wish on anyone. Seeing your baby lying there dying on the inside is more indescribable then I could ever express. The feeling of hopelessness was immediate and overwhelming. *What do we do now? Just wait? Cry?* We were at a loss for thoughts and words.

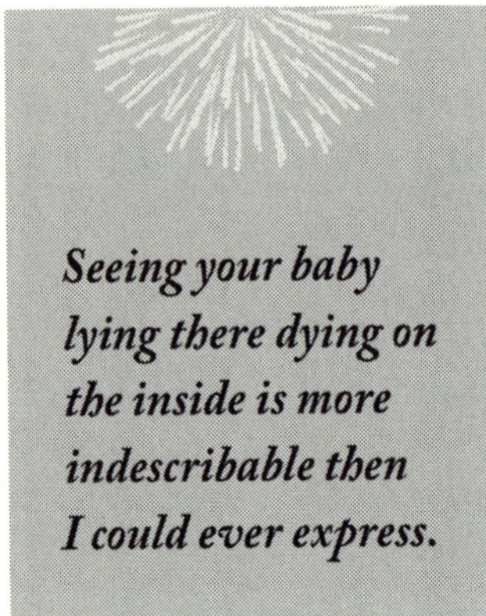

# Chapter 2

# FIRECRACKER BABY

Let's start at the beginning of Ella's story, shall we? Ella Rose McBride was born by cesarean section on July 4, 2005, at 2:00 p.m., weighing in at 7 lbs. 1 oz. As they lifted her slimy little body above the blue dividing sheet so I could see her and announced that she was a girl, I asked Joe, "Does she look like an Ella?" Our eyes filled with tears of joy as Joe responded, "Yes, she does." Her name was confirmed. Our little beautiful, blue-eyed, healthy-looking, firecracker baby arrived to complete

our family. They took my sweet baby away to do all the initial cleaning and testing and pushed my bed to a separate room until I could get the feeling back in my toes. Those minutes seemed like hours as I watched the hands of the clock slowly move by.

Anesthesia doesn't always like me, and once I was wheeled back to my regular room, it hit me hard. Family was entering the room the see the new precious bundle of joy, and there I was puking off the side of the bed with my mom holding the bed pan for me the whole time. I felt like waving to everyone and saying, "Don't mind me over here throwing up in the corner, just love on the baby." Not the way I had it planned in my mind, but things don't always go as *we* have them planned, do they?

Once evening arrived, the vomiting had subsided, and our little family was together welcoming in the new addition. She started out to be an easygoing baby. The next few days were pretty uneventful. All the basic baby testing checked out normal, and Ella was figuring out the whole nursing thing. We were able to go home and have our happily ever after. Wait, is there really such a thing here on earth? I may have thought that at one point in time, but now, I think the only happily ever after is in heaven. Trials came our way, and oh my, we were so not ready for this trial, but the outcome can only be a true testament to God and His love.

Our calm baby girl's doctor appointments seemed to be going smoothly. Even at our six-month appointment with the nurse practitioner, she offered that we could skip the nine-month appointment and just come back for Ella's twelve-month check-up as Ella seemed to be growing well, looking well, and acting well. At about ten months, I started noticing that Ella seemed to stop gaining weight and not hitting the normal milestones for her age. She could sit up fine, and would roll over occasionally, but she didn't really try to crawl to get to things or go anywhere. She was happy where she was. I had stopped nursing at that point, and she just didn't seem too interested in drinking fluids. Only a few ounces now and then. I made the call and the doctor's office was happy to see her and, probably, to see if I was just an overprotective mother. And yes, I am, but with good reason and instincts.

Our pediatrician, Dr. Ho, agreed that Ella seemed to plateau on the growth chart and wanted to see her every couple of weeks to check her weight. He asked that I keep a food diary of what she ate and how many ounces of formula and liquid she consumed. He wanted to make sure that Ella was getting the proper nutrition that she needed. I felt good about the plan. At that point, there still weren't any huge red flags. She still seemed like the same happy-go-lucky baby.

The food diary was underway with the date, the time, what she ate, how much she drank. Day after day, I was religious about keeping the dairy up to date so it could be as accurate as possible. She would only take in about 20 oz. a day but ate pretty well. She liked a variety of baby foods, like carrots and green beans. She was happy to sit in her highchair and try to feed herself. When you keep track and write everything down, it can be eye-opening on how much or how little one intakes. We visited the doctor every two weeks, and Dr. Ho ran some tests to rule out a few obvious things that could be going on. The tests came back negative. A few weeks later, some more tests. Still negative. Nothing major was standing out, other than the fact that she wasn't growing. That was why Dr. Ho was insistent on seeing her often. He told me, "No matter how a baby looks, if they stop

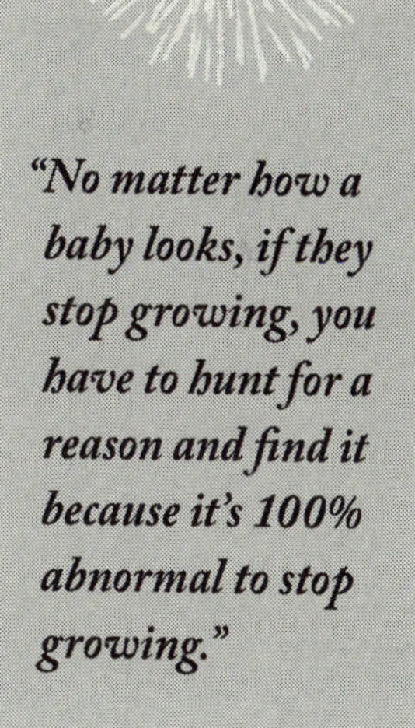

growing, you have to hunt for a reason and find it because it's 100% abnormal to stop growing." The little peanut was only about 16 lbs. She hadn't gained weight since her six-month check-up and was not hitting milestones for her age. When holding her, you could feel her breastbone in her chest as it protruded out and she had these skinny little arms and legs. She just didn't have any meat on her bones. But she was still a smiling, happy, well-behaved, one-year-old.

*God created you on purpose.*

# Chapter 3

# TA-DA!

The evening of July 30, 2006, something was unsettling in my soul. I was overcome with fear and darkness. Ella appeared to have a cold, which was a bit strange for the end of July. I laid my hands on her sleeping, calm body and prayed over her before I went to bed, "Father, please look after Ella and place Your loving arms around her. I don't know what is going on in her little body, but I pray that when I take her to the doctor tomorrow, You will give the doctor wisdom to find what is going on so she may be healed to grow and thrive. I pray this in Jesus' name. Amen." It was a restless night's sleep with the tossing and turning of the unknown in our heads.

On the morning of July 31, 2006, I woke up earlier than normal to check on Ella. Joe and I entered her room and just gazed at her while she lay in her crib sleeping so peacefully with her little fingers curled through the holes of her favorite pink and white crocheted blanket.

She didn't go anywhere without that blankie. It was her comfort item. Ella was a self-soother. She didn't take a pacifier or suck her thumb, but she always did the cutest thing with her tongue to soothe herself. It was like she was suckling with her tongue and her little jaw would move back and forth. At the same time, she would rub the soft corners of her blanket back and forth across her nose ever so lightly. You could always tell when she was tired, because those lips would pucker a bit and that jaw would start to move and before you knew it that blankie was touching her nose.

As she slept with her fingers through the spaces of the crocheted blanket that morning, her breathing seemed more labored then normal. Joe decided he would stay home from work with Noah while I took Ella to the doctor. It sounded like a plan that any family would do for a quick doctor check and maybe a stop by the pharmacy to pick up an antibiotic that might be needed before going about the day.

When Ella and I arrived at the doctor's office, it wasn't super busy. There were only a few people in the waiting area. Our name was called, and we headed back and did the regular weight and length check (which she was getting pretty accustomed to doing by this time), then entered one of the patient rooms with Purdue University posters plastered on the walls. This time seemed different as the nurse kept the pulse oximeter on longer than usual, with no mention as to why. Usually, it was a quick check of oxygen level then the removal of the monitor device. But this time Ella's big toe was lit up like a red Christmas bulb. Her breathing was still labored as I held her and carried her back and forth in the small room. A feeling of anxiousness began to creep up inside me. I think as a mom, a caregiver, God gives you certain instincts and knowledge about the child you are caring for that only you possess. You know when your loved ones are hurting.

*I think as a mom, a caregiver, God gives you certain instincts and knowledge about the child you are caring for that only you possess.*

You know what makes them giggle. You know when they are fibbing and trying to sneak something by you. It's why you can tell them that you have eyes in the back of your head. You've been there, done that, and you know your child. This time was no different. I knew something was wrong, I just didn't know exactly what or how severe. Come to find out, God was the only one who truly knew, and He was in control. He was going to answer my prayer from the night before and give the doctor the wisdom to realize something really wrong was going on and we needed help—God's help, the doctors' help, help from our friends and family.

Dr. Ho entered the room and gave Ella a quick examination. He wanted to do a chest x-ray and, of course, I agreed. He put the order in the computer, and I carried Ella down to the first floor where the x-ray technician met us. In order to get an accurate x-ray of a wiggly toddler, they put her in this body cast looking thing, which no one would enjoy, especially a twelve-month-old, and click went the pictures. Thankfully, it only took a few minutes, and then I was carrying her back up to the second floor again to get the results after the radiologist had reviewed the x-rays. I could tell she was getting sleepy from all the excitement and from not feeling well. "It's okay, baby girl. We will be out of here before you know it." And she laid her head on my chest, clutching her blankie.

Back in the Purdue University swag-filled exam room, we waited patiently for the results. I will never forget the image of Dr. Ho walking in with his Purdue jersey on, hand held high, clasping the x-rays with such a "ta-da" look on his face. They found something! The words coming from Dr. Ho's mouth started to blur the longer he spoke. Was I hearing him correctly?

"The x-rays show that Ella's heart is enlarged. In fact, it is about twice the size it should be," Dr. Ho exclaimed.

*Wait, what!?* My heart sank into my stomach. This numbness came over my body as I pulled Ella tighter against me. On one hand, I had an answered prayer, but at the same time, tears filled my eyes with worry and the thought of, *What does this mean?* He ran through a couple of things that it could be off the top of his head. Dr. Ho was speculating that Ella perhaps had a whole in her heart which was causing improper blood flow. We definitely needed further testing. It did baffle him that she had an enlarged heart as she had never had a heart murmur and no real indications of such a problem. The mystery of her condition was growing. Dr. Ho said that the next step was to send Ella over for an echocardiogram. That test would give us more information and give a closer look at the workings of her heart. It would be performed in another building across town. He assured me that they would call over and have everything ready when we arrived. Once the test was completed, then I would need to bring Ella back to his office for the results.

I'm sure I had a very intense and panicked look on my face. Dr. Ho stated, "Despite how awesome modern medicine is, we still don't have a 'Star Trek scanner' that we can just point at someone and tell us everything going on." He reassured, "We will figure this out." He was very comforting and even offered to call Joe for me and explain what little we knew at this point. I thanked him for the offer, but said I would call him myself. I urgently needed to talk to Joe and to have him there with me at this time. *Okay, I can do this! I can do this! Lord, I need You!!*

I carried Ella to the car, praying the whole way, "Lord, I'm scared! Help us. Wrap Your healing arms around Ella." Once I buckled her in her car seat, I tried to give her a little something to drink, as she hadn't wanted anything all morning. She pushed it away. I let her be and sat in the driver's seat. I took a few deep breaths,

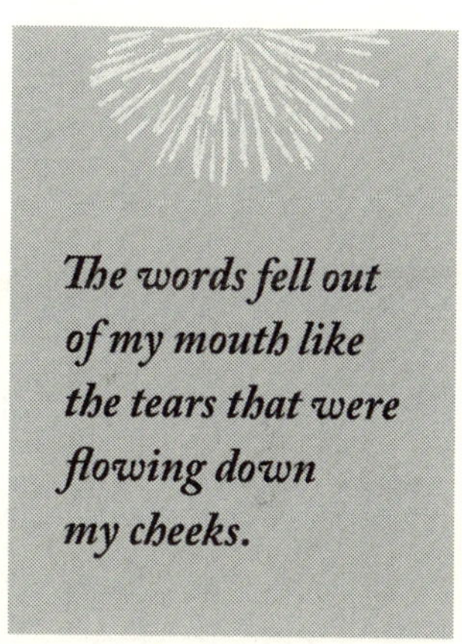

*The words fell out of my mouth like the tears that were flowing down my cheeks.*

hands nervously shaking as I called Joe. Trying my best to compose myself, the words fell out of my mouth like the tears that were flowing down my cheeks. Joe was in complete shock with the news he was hearing and the unknown ahead of us. I could tell the tears were welling up in his eyes, but he was trying to be brave for me.

We decided that I would call my mom to see if she could leave work (she and Joe worked at the same company and location) and come over to the house to watch Noah so Joe could join me. He also wanted to give his mom and dad, Connie and Roy, a call to inform them of the situation. He would meet me as soon as he could at the imaging center where the test was going to be done. I dialed Mom's number, and she answered pretty quickly. With a broken voice, I explained what was going on. I could hear it in her voice that she was fighting back tears as worry consumed her. She said she would be over to watch Noah as soon as she could gather her things. My mom is truly the one of the strongest women I know. I was so thankful that I could rely on her at this time.

While I was on the phone with my mom, Joe called his mom and dad. I know this had to be one of the hardest phone calls he has ever had to make. You see, when Joe was only six months old, he had a six-year-old sister who passed away. Sheryl was born with reverse blood vessels in her heart, and her sweet little heart never worked properly. She was the second born and their first child, Shari, came just eleven months earlier. They were "Irish twins." Needless to say, Joe's mom and dad had their hands pretty full, even without the fact the Sheryl needed constant special care. I recall her sharing stories of when the girls were little and her having some pretty tiring days. It took a long time to feed Sheryl when she was little as everything she did wore her out. Her heart was working overtime. They had a lot of doctor visits and spent a lot of time at Riley Hospital for Children. Doctors tried a new procedure to correct the problem, but, unfortunately, it wasn't a long-term fix. It is so heart-wrenching to hear what they went through. Back then, you couldn't even be in the same hospital room with your child, except for a very short amount of time each day. Connie talked about other parents she would meet and become connected with as they sat in the hallways visiting and sharing stories with each other, waiting for the time they could go in and see their children.

Sadly, in 1973 Sheryl's heart couldn't keep up any longer and she passed away, leaving a lifelong scar on her parents' hearts. Roy and Connie have always said that Ella reminds them of Sheryl, and looking back at old pictures, you can see the resemblance, especially when they were toddlers. They both had fair skin, beautiful round eyes, and sweet demeanors. They have always felt a special connection with Ella through Sheryl. I knew the news of Ella's enlarged heart would bring up memories of their own precious child.

When Joe phoned his mom, Connie fell to her knees with the news, as I am sure she was reliving her own experience and not wanting her grandchild to endure health issues and her son to go through what they had gone through. She wept in disbelief and offered any help that we would need—another one of the strongest women I know. They lived almost three hours away. So, at that moment, knowing how hard it would be, they needed to wait and see what we could find out. Connie graciously offered to let Joe's sister and the rest of the family know what was going on.

"I lift up my eyes to the hills, from where does my help come? My help comes from the Lord, who made heaven and earth."

Psalm 121:1-2 (ESV)

# Chapter 4

# HEART FAILURE?

Finally regaining a little composure, I arrived with Ella at the imaging center, where the registration nurse eagerly awaited our arrival. The nurses were so kind as they escorted us back to the dimly lit room with the echocardiogram machine ready to go. I laid Ella down on the cushioned patient table and removed her shirt for the test. She was a bit squeamish at first when they started the echocardiogram. I'm sure the slimy cool gel that they put on the end of the wand and then on her chest felt cold and weird at the same time, on top of not knowing what the heck was going on. Luckily, she settled down pretty quickly with the bribery of a sucker. A good sucker can solve so many problems. It seemed like an eternity for the testing to be completed. Back and forth over the area of her heart, then stopping at certain places to click the button that would take a snapshot of a specific area and seeing the red and blue blood flow rapidly going through her heart. Hearing her heartbeat and measuring the sounds and waves. I didn't know what any of it meant, but so desperately wanted to. It all looked like a big blob on the screen. I wanted to ask so many questions, but refrained so the nurse could do what she needed to do. I did finally ask if everything was okay. She assured me that the cardiologist in Indianapolis would be able to look over everything and give us some information.

Our sister-in-law happened to be an imaging nurse in the area, and once she heard what was going on, she came right over to see us. It was so good to see a friendly face and have a hug from someone I knew. She also reassured me that the cardiologist in Indianapolis was one of the best, and we would

*Joe scooped Ella up and gave her the biggest hug.*

know something before too long. Joe arrived shortly after the echocardiogram was completed, and I felt the tightest hug we have ever shared. Joe scooped Ella up and gave her the biggest hug as well. She was all snuggled up in her favorite blankie.

We waited around for just a bit as Dr. Steinberg (St. Vincent's Pediatric Cardiologist) was going to review the echocardiogram and make sure he had all the images that he needed before we left the facility.

Once we were given the go ahead, we headed back to Dr. Ho's office to discuss the results and next steps. I didn't want Joe to leave my side, but we had two vehicles and needed to drive them both back to the other office. I prayed the whole way, asking for healing and clarity and wisdom for the doctors. I felt God's hand in the situation and on Ella, even though we still didn't know the severity of her circumstances.

The three of us were silent in the exam room, just waiting for hopeful news. It was mid-afternoon now, and we hadn't eaten since that morning. I didn't feel overly hungry. I think the emotions of the day masked any hunger that might have been there. I tried to give Ella something to eat, some snacks from our diaper bag, but she was not interested in anything. Then Dr. Ho walked into the room, more somber this time. His initial thought of a small opening in her heart didn't appear to be the case. Dr. Ho went

on, "The results from the echocardiogram showed that Ella's heart is functioning at only 10-15%." 10-15%, what does that mean?? "A normal heart functions at 65%," he explained. He added, "Ella is in heart failure."

Heart failure? Heart failure! Both of our hearts sunk at that moment. I could feel the blood drain from my body and needed to sit down as I tried to concentrate on what was being said. *Our baby girl is in heart failure!* How could this have happened and how could we not have known something this major was going on in her body? She looked perfectly fine on the outside but had been slowly dying on the inside.

Ella could feel the tension and sadness from us all in the room. She began to cry. All we could do in the moment was hold her and try to comfort her. All these questions came to mind, and I wanted to blame someone for something and wanted the results to be untrue and to vanish. Ella had been seen by a doctor every two weeks for the last two months. But, there wasn't anyone to blame.

Looking at that precious girl, there was no external sign and really no obvious internal one until she was at her weakest, which prompted further testing to make the discovery.

Thoughts of possible heart surgery and the unknown were being spoken. It was hard to understand it all when I had just brought her in for what appeared to be a cold.

Dr. Ho said that he and Dr. Steinberg consulted, and they felt that Ella needed to be admitted to the hospital at St. Vincent so further testing could be performed to determine what was going on in her little body. Dr. Ho offered to have Ella taken by ambulance, or, if we wanted to run home to pack a few things first, we could take her as long as it was a quick stop. We decided we would like to run home, grab a few things, gather our thoughts, get Noah settled and update everyone on the situation, and then head to Indianapolis. Dr. Ho mentioned we might be in Indianapolis for just a couple of days. Little did we know what was going to transpire next.

"Some of our greatest moments of influence are when others get to watch God walk us through fire."

Unknown

# Chapter 5

# CONTACT THE CHAPLAIN

On the way home, I had to continually wipe the tears away so I could see the road. Mom and Skip (my stepdad) were there, and they were more than willing to take care of Noah as long as needed. I had just started a home-based business a few months earlier and needed to speak with my co-worker to have a few things submitted for me due to the circumstances. I think our minds were in a bit of a fog as we grabbed some food, a couple of changes of clothes, and the essentials and wanted to get to Indianapolis as quickly as possible. And, of course, our family was wanting answers. We were, too, but we just didn't have any to give.

We hugged and kissed Noah goodbye and knew he would be in good hands with Grandma and Grandpa. It was so hard trying to explain to a two-year-old that we had to go away with his sister for a few days and we would miss him. As we traveled down the road, the van was filled with silence between the few phone calls to family and friends. We arrived at the hospital an hour later. We had been instructed to enter through the emergency room doors. Joe offered to drop us off at the door, but I just couldn't be separated from him at the time. I just felt like we needed to stick together. We found a parking

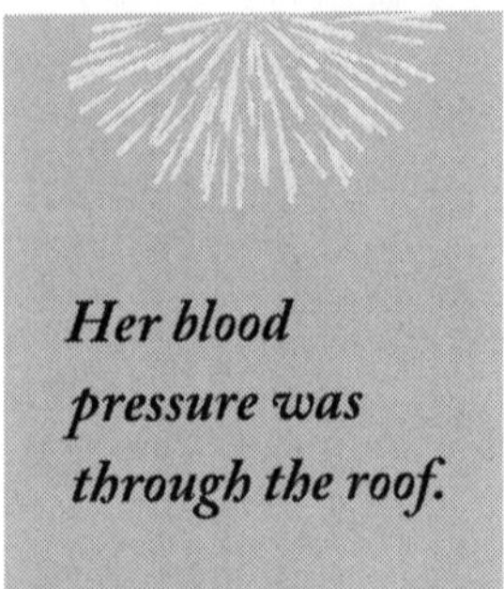

*Her blood pressure was through the roof.*

spot and quickly walked through the emergency room entrance, clutching Ella wrapped in her pink and white blanket. As we walked in, we were greeted by the staff that had been notified that we would be coming. Immediately, they rushed us back to one of the brightly lit rooms where we met Dr. Steinberg, and he starting examining Ella. For the first time, her blood pressure was taken. They wrapped that tiny cuff around her little arm, and I don't think I had ever seen such a small blood pressure cuff. As it worked its way up higher and higher on the monitor screen and finally settled on the numbers, it showed that her blood pressure was through the roof. Over 200! This was a new surprise and mystery to us and the hospital staff. It added to the questions and not the answers. I didn't know anything about blood pressure numbers and what was good versus bad. We quickly learned that over 200 is very, very bad, deathly bad, even for an adult let alone a 16 lb. toddler. Doctors are trained with keeping their composure and not getting freaked out in front of patients and families when circumstances are dire. This can be good in certain situations, but I wanted to know what was going on. If it was bad, tell me!

I held Ella close in my arms as Dr. Steinberg rechecked her blood pressure and expressed that he wanted to do another echocardiogram. By this point, Ella was wiped out even though she slept all the way there. She was tired of being examined and squeezed. As I was holding her, the doctor instructed me to try to keep her as still as possible. Certain things doctors say don't fully compute in the mind when you are dealing with a stressful situation until the true meaning behind things being said comes to light later. With Ella's blood pressure running at such a dangerously high number, Dr. Steinburg was afraid she was going to have a stroke or a heart attack. Any additional stress, like crying for example, would increase her blood pressure that much further to where her body just wouldn't be able to handle it. The anxiety continued to creep up inside me. Was this really happening? *Lord, is this really happening?*

After the second echocardiogram confirmed what the original echocardiogram had shown, Dr. Steinburg started throwing out thoughts of possible kidney problems along with her heart problem. She may need surgery, a possible heart transplant, etc. I felt like I was having an out-of-body experience with all that was being said and all the events of the day. The question, "Why was this happening?" kept coming to mind. Dr. Steinburg told us that he was going to admit Ella to the ICU. They would get her hooked up to an IV and start medicines that would give her body some ease, similar to a medically-induced coma so that her body wouldn't have to work so hard until they could figure out what was going on. They certainly didn't want her to get upset and spike her blood pressure with her heart being so weak.

Dr. Steinburg left the room to get the paperwork started and set things in place to assign Ella a room. Joe and I stood looking at one another, holding Ella in between us, still stunned. One thing I will never forget is overhearing the doctor tell the nurse, "Get an ICU room ready and contact the chaplain to meet the family in the room." I didn't understand the magnitude of those words until much, much later. Again, I was in a bit of a fog, but my thought at the time was that it was very sweet of the doctor to have a pastor to come and pray with us.

At a much later time, my stomach just turned at the realization that the doctor thought that Ella might not make it and that we should have the chaplain to help us through the circumstance. *Deep exhale.*

Joe was holding Ella at this time when my sister, Stacie, and brother-in-law, Jim, walked in. They came straight from work as they lived in the Indianapolis area. As we walked toward each other with arms wide open, I felt as if I just collapsed into Stacie's arms. The day had zapped my energy, and I couldn't contain the tears and worry that were in me any longer. I just sobbed as she squeezed me tightly in her arms. The air in the room seemed to turn cooler. As we were updating Jim and Stacie on the recent findings from Dr. Steinberg, a nurse came in to take Ella so they could get her settled in her room. I know it was so hard for Joe to let go and hand her sleeping body over to the nurse. She looked so sweet and calm, and we didn't want to leave her side.

The ICU doctor appeared at the door and greeted us. He explained they would get Ella all set up in her room and that he would need to put in a central line. This would help with administering medicines and drawing blood when needed. A nurse showed the four of us to a waiting area where there was a computer and information on a site called CaringBridge. Stacie and Jim were kind enough to update immediate family while we looked into what this site was all about. This was before Facebook and all the different social media outlets. At the time, you had to call people or email them if you wanted to communicate. This site allowed us to have a place to journal and keep whoever wanted to know up to date on what was going on with Ella. That was when we wrote our first journal entry. Joe was being so brave and strong and keeping it together for us. He set up the account and helped me put the sentences together.

The site was such a blessing as people were able to leave such encouraging comments and prayers. We quickly learned prayer DOES change things, and we needed all the prayer warriors we could contact. Over time, there were people praying for Ella and all of us from the East Coast to the West Coast. Our relatives around the country shared our prayer requests and Ella's story with their friends, co-workers, church members, and prayer warriors. People we didn't even know and who didn't know Ella were gathering together in prayer for her. We welcomed every one of them.

The rest of the time, we waited impatiently. How was she doing? Was she scared or upset? Some time had passed, and a nurse came to retrieve us. We all walked through the glass doorway into her dim, chilly-feeling room where the curtain was still wrapped around Ella's bed as the doctor was finishing up his work. It certainly smelled like a hospital room. The room was very spacious, with a couch that could pull out into a bed and a private bathroom. The doctor who put the central line in pulled back the curtain and explained that it was done and that Ella had already been given medicine to keep her calm. She laid there so still and so tired from the day. Within a span of a few hours, she had all of these wires and tubes hooked up to her, coming from every part of her body. She had heart monitor leads on her chest, a line in one leg close to her ankle, which was taped to a board so it wouldn't come out if she happened to move around too much, another line in her other leg, a catheter, a blood pressure cuff on her arm, a pulse ox monitor on her big toe, and an oxygen canal in her nose, with the tubes taped to her checks so it wouldn't come out. There were several monitors with different colored lines and numbers, and we didn't know what anything meant at the time, although we would quickly learn what was what and what to look out for. All we could do in that moment was to look at each other and Ella with lost looks on our faces.

*We all circled Ella's bed, joined hands, and she led us in prayer.*

The hospital chaplain entered the room and greeted us. I think she knew the gravity of the situation. We all circled Ella's bed, joined hands, and she led us in prayer. She reassured us that she would check in on us, and if we needed anything, she would be available. It was getting late by this time, so we hugged Jim and Stacie goodnight, and they went on to their home.

A few minutes later, the nurse shared with us that there was a parent room available for us to stay in for the night, if we wished. It was a small room with two twin beds and the essentials for getting some rest. I just couldn't imagine being apart from Ella given the events of the day, so Joe stayed in the parent room, and I slept on the couch in Ella's room. I laid there awake for quite some time, praying, asking the "why" questions, hoping for answers soon, begging that Ella would be okay, reliving the day until I finally drifted off to sleep, emotionally drained.

*"Faith does not make things easier. It makes them possible."*
—Unknown

# Chapter 6

# LONGING TO HOLD HER

Wednesday, August 2, 2006, 11:24 a.m.
Journal entry by Stacie (Angela's sister)

*First of all, thank you to everyone for your support and prayers. We are very blessed to have such wonderful friends and family. Just wanted to give you all an update… many doctors came to visit yesterday. They are testing for everything. Some of the tests they are doing could take up to three or four weeks before they get results. They are very concerned with her blood pressure as it is very high. They have been trying to bring it down slowly so as not to cause any other problems with any of her other organs. She also had fluid in her lungs, so they are giving medicine to help drain this. I will write more when we get more of an update. Please keep praying for Ella.*

Over the next few days, we met with so many different doctors. So many people were baffled by Miss Ella. For doctor after doctor, we repeated what information we knew about Ella and fielded all kinds of questions. Could Ella have contracted something viral? Bacterial? Were Joe and I related before we were married? (The answer was no!) There were constant blood draws, repeat echocardiograms and blood pressure checks, and introduction of new meds. One medicine in particular, the infectious disease doctor called "liquid gold." They just didn't know if Ella had contracted something strange so this was intended to handle anything out of the ordinary. This medicine was a combination of antibodies to help Ella's body. We welcomed anything they could do.

We had so many visitors of family and friends, some whom we hadn't seen in a very long time. There were offers to bring food, care baskets, help in taking care of Noah. Mom was great in handling Noah on the home front. We felt like everything was being taken care of so we could just be and focus on Ella and whatever needs might arise with her. One dear friend gave me a notebook, which became very vital to me, and I am so thankful for the gift. I used it to journal, collect my thoughts, convey my true feelings of despair, jot down which doctors and nurses we came in contact with. I wrote down questions that would come mind so we wouldn't forget the next time we saw the doctor. It was a small lifeline that I desperately needed. She had also gone through a very scary time with her daughter just a few years prior. It's during these times that you need to lean on someone who can help you through

*It's during these times that you need to lean on someone who can help you through these tough situations.*

these tough situations. Someone who can understand what you are going through.

One of the hardest things to handle now that Ella was admitted to the hospital was not being able to hold her. She was hooked up to so many things, and one particular medicine that was administered had to be at a level height with her heart at all times. Modern medicine can be such a mystery on how it works, but we continued to trust the doctors and the efforts they were putting in to discover what was going on in that little body of hers.

I vividly remember on day three, our lovely nurse, knowing the struggle of not being able to hold Ella and desperately wanting to, tried to help me into the bed so I could hold Ella just for a bit. I'm sure that was quite a sight. I climbed onto a chair near the bed and hiked my legs over the "keep you in" bars and then tried to maneuver around all the wires that Ella was hooked up to just so I could wrap my arms around her. It wasn't working out too well. There were just too many wires getting in the way. So, we carefully made our way to the chair, adjusting her medicine dispenser along the way so it was at the same level with her heart as we moved. We finally settled into the chair. To have her in my arms and give snuggles, for just that short bit, was so refreshing. I think she could feel her momma's love.

On day four, the doctor was able to ease up on some of the medicines and Ella was much more alert. We passed our time by singing "You are My Sunshine" and reading books like *Guess How Much I Love You.* Family brought some of her favorite toys, like Baby Tad. That green guy use to crack her up. When his belly lit up and music came from inside, we saw a glimpse of a crooked little smile and a little gleam in her eyes. *There you are!*

She had started eating and drinking again. She would have about an ounce or two of formula at a time and some Cheerios. One day, she attempted to eat part of an apple. I swear the red apple was about as big as her head. Lying in bed, she held it in her grasp with both hands and nibbled away. This was a big task for her. She ate maybe a fourth of it and was done, apple juice all over her checks and chin. It was nice to see her eat something other than a handful of Cheerios.

With the food journal I had been keeping, we realized the reason she hadn't been drinking very much at a time was because everything she did tired her out. With eating, drinking, sitting up, she was doing all her body could do. Sucking on a bottle and swallowing was movement and her body was exerting its energy to do just the basic of tasks. The guilt started to settle in. Probably more for myself than Joe. Being the main caretaker, I was feeling horrible. I was trying to force her to do things that her body just couldn't handle. How could I not have known something major was wrong with my own baby?

*You are beautifully and uniquely made.*

# Chapter 7

# GOD LOVES HER MORE

Thursday, August 3, 2006, 10:43 a.m.
Journal entry by Angela

*Little bit of a rough night—Ella became a little restless and was trying to roll over in bed. I was trying to keep her lying on her back due to all the wires. Her blood pressure was spiking up around 170, and then she threw up. The nurse gave her something to calm her down. Thankfully that helped, and she was able to sleep through the night. They did a chest x-ray this morning. Joe just came, and they are going to do another echocardiogram, so I will write more later.*

Friday, August 4, 2006, 12:14 a.m.
Journal entry by Joe

*Hey folks…Joe here. Just want to add a quick note before signing off for the day. We are seeing your prayers working for Ella as she truly is getting stronger. Angela commented earlier that she is smiling, talking, flirting, playing peek-a-boo, all that fun stuff. Things that just melt your heart. She was up today from around 4:00 until around 10:00 or so. I think since she was able to eat a nice lunch and dinner today, her energy is increasing and perhaps beginning to fight back. It's incredible to see so many friends and family come together in Christ in prayer. Angela and I are praying for God's will here, whatever He has planned for us. We welcome it with open arms. Of course, we love that little thing with all our hearts and then some. But, you know God loves her more than that, more than we can fathom. God had a plan for her before she was born. I believe, through her, God is at work here. He is reaching out to everyone who receives her news and falls to their knees. This is how He works, people. It's taken me some time during this experience to truly realize that. Earthly feelings want her to get better, and I certainly do. More than that, God's will is being witnessed, and we cannot know what that is. So, we are praying that we get closer to God through Jesus because He paid the ultimate sacrifice. He paid it in advance for this right here, so that we may be comforted in knowing that God has Ella in the palm of His hands. His love is pure, unlike ours. He is the light. God bless all of you. Your words of encouragement and prayers are not going unnoticed. Love all of you. ~Joe*

Joe's words ring so true but can be so hard to truly comprehend with our worldly mind and flesh. God does love Ella more than we do, and He loves us more than anyone else can. We would like to think that the love we have for our children and the love we pour into them is more than anyone else ever could. But God is the Almighty, and we are all His children first. During this time in our lives, I didn't quite see it that way. I certainly could not wrap my mind around the thought of God taking her and her not being here on earth with us. I think Joe and I were preparing differently. He was preparing that God's will might not be to heal her here on earth, but still holding on to hope. I was holding on to the

selfish desires of my heart and praying that God wouldn't take our baby girl away. We were seeing little miracles every day with her slowly gaining strength and life flowing back into her body.

*"If God brings you to it, He will bring you through it."*
—Unknown

# Chapter 8

# MOVING TO RILEY HOSPITAL

On the morning of day five, Dr. Steinburg surprised us when he entered the room. He completed a quick exam on Ella, then sat down and wanted to chat. He started to explain that he felt as if something was going on with Ella's kidneys in addition to her heart. He felt it would be best for her to be transferred to Riley Hospital for Children, which was about 10 miles away. *WHAT? Move to another hospital?*

I so appreciated his demeanor at the time, though. I felt like he was talking to us like real people, not just as the parents of a patient. He explained that they did not have a nephrologist (kidney specialist) on staff at the moment, and he really felt like that was what Ella needed. Riley Hospital would be able to provide that and perform the proper testing that she would need. And since she was more stable, she would be able to handle the transfer over to the other hospital. With all that had been thrown at us over the past few days, we were overwhelmed and looked to Ella's pediatrician for advice. We trusted Dr. Steinburg, as we could tell that he had Ella's best interest in mind, but at the same time we needed confirmation from another doctor, too. We called Dr. Ho, and he was completely on

board with Dr. Steinburg, so we started the transfer process. The doctors at St. Vincent were a huge part of saving Ella's life, and we will forever be grateful for how they helped her. It really was a miracle that she was responding so well to the medicines. Now we need to move forward to find out the cause of her problems. Once everything was in order, they were going to take her over by ambulance, and I told them that I wanted to ride with her. The poor thing was already scared enough.

My friend, Shelby, had already contacted me that day and wanted to come for a visit, which I absolutely welcomed. But a lot had transpired in a short amount of time, and I felt so bad for my dear friend as she was coming to visit us, and I had no idea when we would be leaving to move over to Riley. She entered the room with my favorite drink, a supportive smile on her face, and a big hug. Shortly after her arrival, the nurse came in and said it was time to go. I know Shelby completely understood, but I still felt bad about the timing and all the effort she had made to come visit when we only got to see her for a minute. That was a very treasured moment though, as sometimes, you just need a hug.

The ambulance crew came in and prepped Ella for the move. There were so many wires and equipment that needed to be in just the right place for the transfer. They wheeled her down the hallway and into the long elevator. I had only been in a standard elevator before, so it was strange to be in one so long that the hospital bed and other people could fit in it all at once. With Ella's little hand wrapped around my finger, we made it down to the large ambulance bay. Squeezing

my finger to the very last second, Ella was rolled into the back of the ambulance. I so wanted to jump in the back with her, but only the EMTs were allowed to ride in the back. I knew she was in good hands, but she was looking around with those bright blue eyes with a look of, "What the heck is going on?"

I had the pleasure of riding shotgun with the driver. I had not ridden in the front part of an ambulance before, and it was quite the experience, especially with the lights flashing and sirens blaring and passing stopped vehicles along the roadway. Again, another one of those moments where you only later realize how intense the situation really was.

Once we arrived at Riley, it was another whirlwind of meeting new doctors and nurses and wondering what they knew, what we needed to do now, and praying that an answer was in the near future. They were quickly getting Ella all settled into her new room on the Pediatric Intensive Care Unit. I have to admit, the move to Riley was scary for me. It looked different and smelled different. They were so much busier with four times the occupancy of

St. Vincent, and the room was so much smaller and looked older and outdated. It didn't have a place for me stay with Ella. The questions ran through my mind. *Did we make the right choice in moving her? Can they really help her here?* I had to cast my doubts aside. *God's got this!* I repeated in my mind. Joe arrived and squeezed my shoulder as a sign that things were going to be okay.

Ella was actually looking a bit better. She was sitting up and suckling while holding on to her blankie (which was really needing to be washed by now, but I wouldn't dare take it from her hands). She did start to get a bit antsy while we waited for the new cardiologist to come and examine her. We gave her Joe's glasses and phone to play with until we could bring up a couple of her toys. She was trying to wear Joe's glasses, but they were so big on her that they just sat crooked on her little face and her eyes looked even bigger than ever. Then she opened up his flip phone and started pushing buttons and put one end up to her ear. She babbled a bit. We said to each other that she was trying to call someone to break her out of the joint—sending an S.O.S. to Mamaw and Papaw.

*He locked eyes with Ella, paused for a second, then did a double-take at his chart.*

The on-call cardiologist walked quickly into the room, followed by an ICU nurse. He locked eyes with Ella, paused for a second, then did a double-take at his chart. He walked to the side of the bed and looked at us. He started to examine her and explained, "Based on the information in her chart, I wasn't expecting her to look this well or be able sit up." This again just confirmed the mystery of what was going on inside her and that she looked perfectly normal on the outside. The body is an amazing thing. She had such the fight to live. After the cardiologist examined her, I really felt that he was in disbelief about what was in her chart. He ordered another echocardiogram and similar tests that St. Vincent had repeatedly done. They needed to do their own testing and needed to see if anything had changed over the past few days.

The doctor left for a short period of time, then returned with the echocardiogram machine. I think Ella was getting use to the cool jelly goop on the end of the wand. She laid pretty still with her blankie in hand, just looking at each one of us hovered around her bed in the now dimly-lit room. This echocardiogram confirmed the previous findings. Her numbers may have increased just a tad, but she was still in heart failure.

The cardiologist explained that they would continue with blood and urine tests at this time. A nephrologist would stop by over the weekend to review her case. With it being a Friday afternoon, they would probably hold off on an MRI or CAT scan until Sunday or Monday, when the experts would be able to review. It seems weird that a hospital would slow down on the weekend, but unless it is an emergency they hold off until the weekdays. Thankfully at this point, Ella was stable. She was on three different types of blood pressure medicines and medicines to help her heart beat easier. The doctor was happy to see that her blood pressure was in a safer range.

**Friday, August 4, 2006**
**Angela's Personal Journal**

*I still can't believe we are here. Since Ella is acting a little bit like herself, it doesn't really feel like anything is wrong with her. I just wish I could take this away from her or give her my heart if they would let me. I really hope and pray the doctors find the problem soon. The wait is so hard. I want to get the healing process started for her so we can take her home.*

*I think the toughest part was the doctor saying she was in heart failure. I love that little girl so much. I can't imagine life without her.*

"TRUST IN HIM AT ALL TIMES, YOU PEOPLE; POUR OUT YOUR HEARTS TO HIM, FOR GOD IS OUR REFUGE."
PSALM 62:8 (NIV)

# Chapter 9

# WHAT WE KNOW SO FAR

The first night at Riley was fairly restful. The nurses found a cushy recliner to bring into the room so I could stay with Ella. I just couldn't bear the thought of being separated from her, especially in a new place. Poor Joe had to put together a makeshift sleeping area in the family waiting room. By the time he went down there to turn in for the night, there were already several others who had staked their claim on the couches and most chairs. He was surprised to see so many people in there and was saddened with what they must be going through. He made do, but I think it was a rough night.

Ella was allowed to see a few visitors at a time. Since it was the weekend, we were showered with visitors. It was such a welcome sight to see and a nice distraction from what was really going on. I think Joe and I both felt stronger being around people, instead of the constant questions and worry swirling around in our heads. Ella was loving all the attention. Noah was also. He had spent the week with Grandma and Grandpa, and I am sure he was a bit spoiled. He probably wore them out at the same time as he was a very active little guy.

I was greeted with a big surprise when I saw him in the waiting area. He had gotten quite the haircut. My mom has always been one for short hairdos. Although, I loved his wispy blonde locks, apparently Noah was looking a bit shaggy, so she had given him a haircut. With his new 'do, he looked as if he had aged two years. Haircut aside, I knew he was being well taken care of.

We walked Noah down the long, bright beige hallway from the waiting area to see Ella. When he walked into the room, the first thing he said with such an innocent tone was, "What happen?" It was one of his favorite phrases.

We explained that Ella was sick and that she was there to get better. When she was better, she would be able to come home. All the sounds and machines in the room didn't seem to phase Noah. I think he would have climbed into the bed with Ella if we would have let him. It was so uplifting to have our little family together for a short time. As Noah was walking out the door, he turned and looked at Ella and said, " I love you." My heart melted at that moment as I tried to hold back tears.

This week was going to be another fun one for Noah as Mamaw and Papaw (Joe's parents) were going to watch him and were sweet enough to come up and stay at our house and take care of things on the home front. And, I have to admit that both grandmas did a great job with potty training. It had been a rough go at it for me, but they were rockin' it.

Late afternoon, we shared a special visit with Joe's Mamaw Alta. She brought a special little bottle of anointing oil and wanted to say a blessing over Ella. As we surrounded Ella's bed and she gazed at each one of us, Alta placed some of the anointing oil on her finger and rubbed it on Ella's forehead. We lifted Ella up in prayer and felt such love in the room. As the day drew to an end and the visitors went home, it was time to refocus on what was going on in front of us.

The next day, we were able to meet one of the doctors who became very impactful in our journey. Dr. Andreoli was the kidney specialist on call, and we were anxious to meet her, especially since Dr. Steinberg had felt that something was going on with Ella's kidneys and she should see a nephrologist. You could hear her approaching down the hallway by the click of her high-heeled shoes. Short in stature and serious in demeanor, Dr. Andreoli's presence entering the room was intimidating. But this

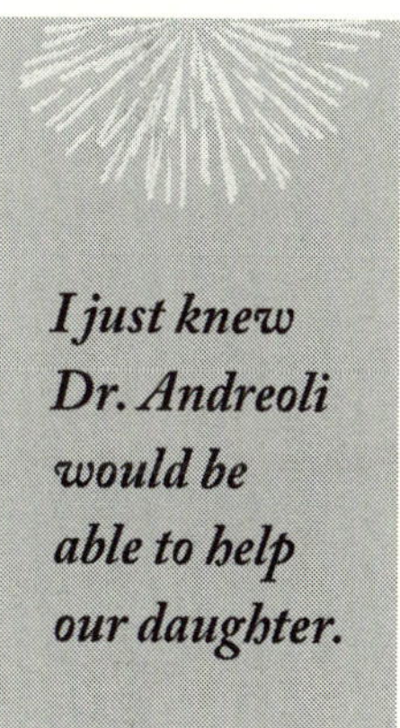


feeling of relief fell upon my shoulders as I just knew Dr. Andreoli would be able to help our daughter.

Dr. Andreoli recalls, "When Ella first presented with severe hypertension, the most important aspect of her initial care was to get her blood pressure under control and find the cause of her severe high blood pressure. Because she had likely been hypertensive for a while, her blood pressure had to be reduced gradually as a sudden drop in her blood pressure to normal would likely be very detrimental to several of her organs, including her kidneys, heart, and brain. So, we worked to gradually reduce her blood pressure and began searching for the cause of her high blood pressure."

*Searching for the cause…* We were longing for answers.

Sunday, August 6, 2006, 7:11 p.m.
Journal entry by Angela

*A few updates… they did a CAT scan today. The initial review did not show anything abnormal. The final review and analysis will be done tomorrow. It has just been a tough day of waiting. More tests should be done tomorrow. They were able to wean her off of the Nipride blood pressure medicine, which was on a pump, so since she is stable they may be able to move her out of the PICU to a step-down intensive care room in the near future. She is still on two blood pressure medications.*

*Just a quick recap—the issues we are dealing with and they are investigating are: **1) cardiomyopathy, 2) high blood pressure**, which they are leaning toward as the cause of the cardiomyopathy, **3) hypotonic, 4) developmental delay/failure to thrive**. Sorry for all of the medical terms. A normal heart works on a 65% basis and from the echocardiograms, they believe hers is running between 10-15%. This just baffles me, especially the way she is acting. They are happy with the range of her blood pressure at this time. They stated today that they would like the top number to stay between 80-120. I really think the control of the blood pressure has made her feel better.*

*Again, I cannot thank you enough for all the outpouring of support. Mom printed off the guestbook so we would be able to read the comments in our room whenever we need to.*

*One of us will be able to stay at the Ronald McDonald house tonight. Everything they have available for families of patients is amazing. A clean shower, nice bed. Even if you don't get a room, you still have access to a kitchen, a quiet room, and food pantry to make your own meal. What a wonderful option in a time like this. You never realize what an organization does until you have to utilize it yourself.*

*We will check in tomorrow. I have my list of questions ready for the doctors.*

*Blessings, Angela*

"Be strong and courageous.
Do not be afraid or terrified
because of them, for the Lord
your God goes with you; he will
never leave you nor forsake you."

Deuteronomy 31:6 (NIV)

# Chapter 10

# WE ARE ALL GROWING

Monday, August 7, 2006, 1:34 p.m.
Journal entry by Joe

*Hello, everyone. I have to say that it's hard to believe that it's been a week already. I'm starting to lose sense of days and time and starting to feel we've been waiting forever. But…today is a brand-new start to the week. God certainly has provided for everyone…and I mean everyone!! I'm honest in saying that my eyes have been opened. I've sat in church and listened intently to what messages are being taught. I've sat in church and listened to the wonderful music and hymns. I've listened to others share their personal experiences of the Lord in their lives. But, I wasn't fully dedicating my life to the Lord. He brought Ella in our lives so that we may witness His love and power. Reading all your words of encouragement and prayers on the CaringBridge site, it moves me. I can't help but tear up every time I have a second to read them…and I do read them all. I opened up my Bible, and it still has a church bulletin. The message that day came from Ephesians 4:6. It reads, "One God and Father of all, who is over all, in all, and living*

**He brought Ella in our lives so that we may witness His love and power.**

*through all" (NLT). We have not been attending that church all that long. The church believes we are all growing followers of Christ. As God is in Ella and us…we are all growing.*

*Ella had some testing this morning, and when she got back, she was able to eat breakfast. She scarfed down one scrambled egg, one and a half French toast sticks, and some of my orange. Then, she was in the mood to have a good time. In fact, such a good time, I had to fully close her door because nurses were peeking their head in and saying we were just having too much fun. She was laughing and cackling so loud. We had the biggest smiles on our faces to hear her laugh like that again.*

*Thank you again to everyone who has offered help in all kinds of ways. And thank you is just not big enough for how Angela and I feel about you all. Now…get off the website and get back to work! Hehe  ~ Joe*

I was thankful that I could go down with Ella while they did the kidney testing. Ella looked a bit nervous as they wheeled her into the long elevator where there were new colors on the walls and new hospital smells. I didn't know what to expect with these tests. The room where they performed the kidney ultrasound was dark with just a small light on and the glow of the ultrasound machine. It was a calming atmosphere. It took about twenty to thirty minutes to capture the pictures for the doctor. It reminded me a lot of the echocardiogram, except it was of her kidneys, measuring size and blood flow to each side. Ella laid very still through it all. We made sure we were able to bring her soft blanket along for support.

The next room for the renal scan was much different. It was very bright and chilly. There was a long machine that Ella had to lay on. She needed to lie very still for this test, and they had to administer fluid so that her kidneys had something to filter and go to her bladder. This test took about an hour or so—not the easiest of feats for a thirteen-month old toddler who had just completed a previous, you-need-to-be-still test. Luckily, she handled it like a champ. It may have been another story if she hadn't had her blankie with her. I was able to help keep her calm by singing songs and reading a few books to her while she suckled and rubbed her nose with her blankie. I could see some images on the machine screen as the test ran, but I had no idea what they meant. They looked like a bunch of white dots appearing in the shape of disfigured beans, more dots on one side than the other. Once everything was done, it was back to the room and the waiting game for the results, fingers crossed that we would receive some answers soon.

*"God, you don't need me but somehow you want me."*
**Lyrics from "Control" by Tenth Avenue North**

# Chapter 11

# OH, THE LITTLE RED WAGON

On Tuesday, Ella graduated to the heart floor. A joyful peace entered our bodies as we felt like this was a huge answered prayer and that Ella was out of the deepest of valleys. The thought of losing her had seeped away. We were still in the valley but a different level. We felt like we were moving in the right direction. There were other patients who had been on the heart floor for weeks, and one little girl in particular for months. That sweet thing had been in and out of the hospital pretty much her whole life. Her room was decorated with girly things and coloring pages, and she knew all the nurses and they all knew and loved her. I didn't really get to spend time with her, but she had an impact on me. Some of the bravest kids you will ever meet have dealt with some of the biggest trials in life. Here we were, new to all this scariness and new to the heart floor, and some of these kids had been battling heart issues for years. The wonder hit me, *What is the plan for Ella's future? How many times will we be here?* We weren't the only ones in this situation and the angst of the unknown.

This room was much bigger than the ICU room. It had its own bathroom, closet, recliner, comfy couch that pulled down into a bed, and our own phone. We could both stay with Ella if we needed to. Joe at this point had been traveling back and forth to home. It gave him a chance to spend some time with Noah and also catch up on some work. I'm sure it was challenging for him, feeling like he needed to be in multiple places at the same time.

Being on a new floor meant meeting new floor doctors and nurses. The cardio group was still large in numbers. This consisted a group of about eight to ten people—students, residents, all in different phases of their college track. Riley was a teaching hospital and boy were they learning a lot. As they surrounded Ella's bed, she would just look at each one of them as they discussed her case. I can only imagine the thoughts going through her head. *Who are you? Why are you all wearing the same clothes [white jackets]? And why are you staring at me?*

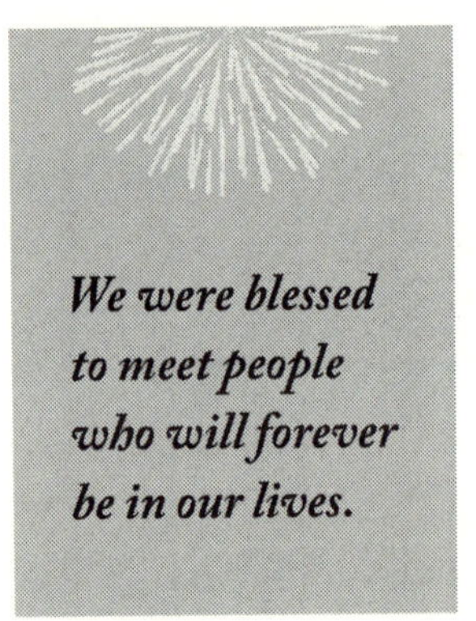



We were blessed to meet people who will forever be in our lives and have helped us so much through this journey. A couple of the nurses we first met were Anna and Alisha. Anna happened to be a friend of a friend that I had known forever. It was nice to see a friendly face and have something in common to chat about other than the stresses facing us. Another nurse that Ella just fell in love with was Alisha. They just bonded immediately. Watch out if Anna and Alisha were working the same shift on the same day, because there was a battle at the nurse's station of who was going to take care of Ella for the day. When you see the same nurses caring for your child and the love and compassion that they pour into children, they find a special place in your own heart. I am so thankful for all the nurses who cared for Ella.

Ella had a few rough nights on the new floor. Her sleep just wasn't the same, and it was harder to entertain her in the bed as she was more alert. Alisha found that Ella had popped a stitch where the arterial line was placed. This had been placed to keep a constant gage of her blood pressure as it was critical at the time. The doctors agreed it was time to remove the arterial line, and they would check Ella's blood pressure every couple of hours with a blood pressure cuff and machine. It was nice to have one less line to worry about and untangle. We were just praying that this way of checking her blood pressure would be easy on her and accurate.

Although she was still hooked up to heart monitors, a central line, and an IV for hydration, with the arterial line out, we were able to take Ella out of her bed and hold her for short amounts of time. What a freeing experience! It really felt like being able to cradle her all over again. I sat in the rocking chair with her on my lap playing with Baby Tad and reading books for about thirty minutes before Alisha appeared at the door and thought Ella might be up for a little ride and a change of scenery. Joe and I were absolutely up for a change of scenery. The thought of being free and Ella well enough to roam the hospital stunned me. Then, Alisha wheeled in the cute little red wood slatted wagon.

*Oh, the little red Riley wagon.* It is the symbol for the hospital. All the wagons are donated from different individuals, organizations, schools, and businesses. They are lined up at the entrances of the hospital, so when you enter with your child, the child can be toted about in a fun wagon. They are also on several floors, for the enjoyment of the kiddos who are able to get out of their rooms. We lined the wagon with a blanket and a couple of pillows so Ella would be snug and comfy. We grabbed the pole with her IV and heart monitor, wheeled it beside the wagon, and off we went. Such a joyous feeling came over us as we walked down the hall, Ella's face smiling when just a week earlier she was barely holding onto life.

We went downstairs and ate some lunch at the cafeteria and saw the huge stuffed animals sitting all along the edges of each floor in the atrium—Winnie the Pooh, Snoopy, a big lion, and a giraffe, just to name a few. On one of the walls there was a huge picture dedicated to Ryan White who spent a lot of his time at Riley when he was ill with AIDS. Also, a beautiful bronze statue of James Whitcomb Riley, who the hospital was named after.

A bricked area through the middle of the open atrium had a stream of water flowing with lots of coins settled at the bottom. You could tell a lot of wishes had been made here. We added some pennies to the mix along with our own wishes.

At one end of the atrium there were two glass elevators. We couldn't resist hopping on. Ella giggled at seeing the objects get bigger and smaller as we went up and down. It didn't take much to amuse us at this point. I hadn't seen this part of the hospital yet, as I really hadn't left the room. We enjoyed that change of scenery, but it was time to head back to the room for a blood pressure check.

*CaringBridge guest post: "How can we say how much you and your family mean to us? It is truly hard to put into words. Please know that our thoughts and prayers are with you all. Remember Philippians 4:13, 'I can do all things through Christ who strengthens me.'"*
—**Michael, Janis, Gabi, and Sofia**

# Chapter 12

# DOTS

Dr. Andreoli visited to share the results of the kidney testing. I was ready to hear some good news and hopefully learn some answers. The renal scan showed loss of function to her kidneys, more on the left side than the right side, meaning they were not working like they should. Another piece to the puzzle. Dr. Andreoli said there was definitely something going on with Ella's kidneys, but still was not sure what. Her urine tests were coming back irregular also. I felt like air was seeping out of a balloon. Her heart was not working right, and now her kidneys. Frustration rose with every disappointing test result. It did click to me what I had seen on the screen during the kidney scan. The dots represented how her kidneys were working, and the reason I didn't see as many dots on the left side was because her left kidney wasn't working as well as the right kidney.

With more testing came more questions. Our medical student tried to prepare us that sometimes there just aren't answers to why things happen. This was such a hard pill for me to swallow, especially with all that is available in the medical community. How could some things just happen and not have an answer for why? With all the technology of today, how can there still be things they just don't know about the body? This is astounding! We had to come to the realization that God is the only all-knowing one, and we had to continue to trust in Him. He had brought us this far, and we had to believe He would carry us the rest of the way.

Another big move being made was the removal of the central line and IV. The central line did allow them to draw blood and administer medicine when needed, but it had been in long enough and needed to be removed to avoid risk of infection. With this being done, Ella was freed up from another major tube being in her body, but this also meant that they would have to manually draw blood from her each morning and that we needed to transition to giving her medications orally. It was also time for the IV fluid to be removed. With this being done, she would need to start drinking more fluids so she would not become dehydrated. With new milestones came new challenges. My baby girl was doing better, and I couldn't have been more thankful for that. At the same time, the fear of how long this was going to last if they couldn't find the problem kept creeping up in the back of my mind.

Miss Ella was not a fan of drinking enough fluids. We were trying everything—milk, juice, water. It was a constant battle throughout the day. I would sneak that bottle in her mouth while she was playing with something. She would take a few sips, then push it away. Round and round we would go. The same with the medicines. They were not the best smelling things, so I am sure they were not the best tasting. Oh, the look on her face when we would put the oral syringe into her mouth. She would suckle for a second, then realize, "Yuck, I don't want to drink that!" But, it was something we HAD to do, and she would have to get use to taking the medications. The struggles of our future days were becoming more apparent.

There were continued talks about doing an MRA/MRI in the near future. A discussion would have to be had with the anesthesiologist to confirm that Ella could handle anesthesia for that long of a period. New doctors continued to get involved in our "case." They were scheduling an ophthalmologist to come by and examine Ella as they needed to rule out any eye damage from her having such high blood pressure—something I wouldn't have even thought of. It would make sense that she could have had blurred vision. Maybe that was why cartoons and colorful shows never caught her attention. She couldn't see them clearly? We take for granted so many things each day, one being how intricately our bodies are made. We don't see the process that is going on inside that allows us to see, hear, move, and live.

*We take for granted so many things each day, one being how intricately our bodies are made.*

**Thursday, August 10, 2006, 11:16 p.m.**
**Journal entry by Angela**

*Ella is sleeping peacefully tonight. The ophthalmologist examined her and didn't see any sign of eye damage at this time. So thankful for that! She still could have had blurred vision at times but no damage.*

*We have found that Ella likes chocolate-flavored carnation drinks. Finally, something we can work with. We were able to get her to drink just enough today (about 8 oz.) so they wouldn't have to put a tube in her nose for extra fluids. She is*

*still eating well. The doctors are still working with getting the right dosage of blood pressure meds for her as they are gradually bringing it into a safe range.*

*A dear friend helped me out today by explaining maybe it is not the why to ask, but the what and how? What will I take from this and how does this change me and make me a better person? I really needed that perspective. This has forever changed our family, and I know I am changed from it.*

*I wonder how this will mold Ella. A med student on the cardio team was saying today how cute Ella was (well, duh) and how she had an intelligent look in her eyes. We think she is going to grow up and solve the mystery as to the source of her problem. I plan to make a special album for Ella to cherish and feel the love of all the friends, family, and people that have never met her face to face.*

*Thanks again, Angela*

With the continued testing and unknown, we clung to the CaringBridge guest posts to lift us up and give encouragement. A few that we cherished read as follow:

*"I find myself praying without even realizing I'm praying. Joe and Angela, our hearts are with you constantly. May God give you strength when you're tired, understanding to our little Noah, a special guiding hand for all the doctors, but most of all may He wrap His loving arms around precious Ella and make her better. We love you all so much!"*—Shari (Joe's sister), Greg, Dustin, and Logan

*"Joe and Angela, you are in our thoughts and prayers. If we can do anything, let us know. Trust in God for He has a plan for you. Thank Him for the many blessings He has given you. Keep the faith. Jesus loves you."*—Love, Dick, Beth, and family

# Chapter 13

# THERE'S A NEW DOCTOR ON THE FLOOR

With the new doctor rotation, we were introduced to Dr. Darragh. He became a very pivotal person in our lives. Such a great thinker! He is tall in stature, balding a bit, and not a man of too many words. You can tell he is always thinking of a solution and has the biggest heart you can find in a doctor. Sometimes, it was hard to know what he was thinking because he is not an overly animated person, but he sure does know his stuff. Dr. Darragh recalls, "The most obvious problem was that her heart function (mainly the left ventricle) was severely below normal.

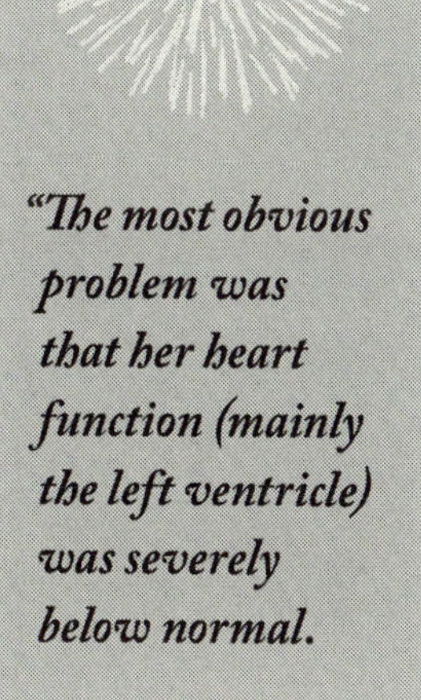

*"The most obvious problem was that her heart function (mainly the left ventricle) was severely below normal.*

As we started to do studies to see why her heart function was weak, it was unusual how her left ventricle was also thicker than normal." He definitely felt that an MRA/MRI was the route to go next, and he was in close contact with Dr. Andreoli.

Because Ella was at least stable right now, there were talks of letting us take her home in the near future. This absolutely terrified me. I couldn't fathom the thought of being her full-time caregiver knowing that we still had a long road ahead of us in trying to find out what was wrong with her. The nurses tried to help me in taking Ella's blood

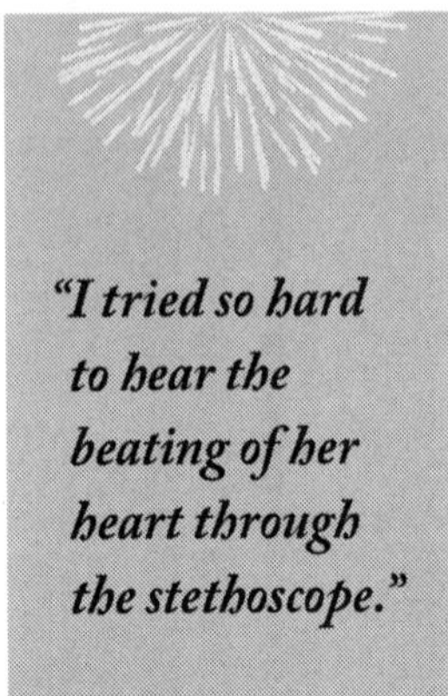



pressure, and I just couldn't do it. I tried so hard to hear the beating of her heart through the stethoscope, but it was so faint, I wasn't catching it in time to get an accurate reading. I told Dr. Darragh my worries, and he agreed with me that it was even challenging for him to hear it as she was so little. So their plan of attack was to try to locate a small portable blood pressure machine that we could use at home. There were no guarantees at this point. We would have to see what they could come up with. I trusted that the Lord was going to lead us in the right direction and guide me with her blood pressure readings.

Early one morning, I was awakened by Ella fussing. It was about 4:30 a.m. There were two nurses standing over her. I have to admit that they weren't our comfort nurses that we were used to. Still good, just not the ones that we had connected so closely with in that short time-frame. I jumped up and hurried over. One of the nurses explained they needed to get the daily blood draw, but they were having difficulty. They couldn't find a good vein that would hold up. We were guessing that Ella was a bit dehydrated. They finally found a vein that looked good, but it was definitely in a spot that I wasn't expecting: her forehead. That's right, her forehead! I asked, "Are you sure that is the best place?" They assured me it was, and sometimes you have to do what you have to do in order to get things done. "Okay, then," I said. I held Ella's head and calmly sang, "You are my sunshine," in her little ear as they stuck the needle in her forehead. The shocked look on her face said it all as her eyes widened. The sound of a cry was building up in her and finally came out. Holding her head still was no small feat. Thankfully, it was over shortly, and she was able to relax quickly. My heart was racing at trying to imagine how that felt for her.

Once the nurses left, we tried to get some rest. I desperately wanted Ella to go back to sleep because we had a big day ahead of us with testing. She wouldn't be able to eat or drink before the test, so I wanted her to sleep in as long as possible. I was able to rock her a bit, and she fell back asleep after the traumatic head poke.

There really isn't a chance to sleep in too late at a hospital. Things start moving and doctors have rounds to do. You never know exactly what time they will be by, but it was my desire to be at the end of the rotation today. I carried Ella around the room, danced, sang songs, trying to keep her mind off of wanting something to eat or drink. A dear friend gave us a CD of a newer Christian band, Casting Crowns. "LifeSong" became our go-to song with Ella. As the words filled the room, we slowly danced to the soft music. It brought such a peace over us.

We also found a fun channel on the television of fish swimming. It was the only channel that finally caught Ella's attention. The hospital had several large fish tanks throughout the first floor, and they put a camera in one of them and live-streamed it on one of the TV channels. It really made for a good distraction. We saw lots of "Nemos."

We were met with the slew of doctors on the cardiology team again. We were all hoping that the MRA/MRI would prove beneficial and give us some answers that we were desperately seeking. The plan for the day was an echocardiogram, confirmation with the anesthesiologist, and if all was okay, then the big test.

**Monday, August 14, 2006**
**Angela's Personal Journal**

*MRI had called around 12:00 stating they could take you—but you hadn't had the echocardiogram yet. The nurse said it was okay, but I reminded her that you were supposed to have the echo first. She double-checked, and I was correct. They needed to know the condition of your heart before trying to do the MRI. I have found that you really have to be your own advocate. I couldn't imagine not being here and not asking questions or not knowing what is going on. Someone has to stay on top of it. They have several patients to tend to, and I have you.*

*A doctor hurried in and did the echocardiogram. The anesthesiologist gave the okay for the MRA/MRI.*

*My heart was pounding so fast as they wheeled you away for the test. We are anxiously waiting to hear the result of the MRA and MRI.*

Ella was gone for a few hours, which felt like an eternity. We hadn't been apart for a long period of time since she was admitted to the hospital. I gasped as I saw the bed come around the corner of the room. I was excited for her return and to know that she was okay. She rested the remainder of the day, and we would most likely have to wait until the following day to find out information on the test results. We were thankful that Ella's heart was strong enough the handle this vital test. As we would soon find out, it certainly was a vital test indeed.

*"You are unique, you know. You need to play it for all it is worth."*—Dr. Darragh

# Chapter 14

# ANSWERS

Tuesday, August 15, 2006, 10:00 p.m.
Journal entry by Angela

*We have had some prayers answered! Something was found—the results from the MRA/MRI indicate that Ella has what is called Abdominal Aorta Stenosis. I am so thankful that they went through with the MRA/MRI. The med student even said today that a higher being must have been helping out on this one. I will attempt to explain the best I can. The aorta (large artery going from the heart down the abdomen) is supposed to be 6mm in width for her size, which Ella's is until it gets right about where the renal arteries branch off and go to the kidneys. At this point, they are guessing it narrows to about 2 mm. Not sure the length that is 2 mm, but then it opens back up and continues to the arteries in the legs. This narrowing is causing less blood flow to the area where the renal arteries draw blood, which in turn makes the kidneys think there is not enough blood, thus making the whole body work harder to try to get more blood flowing. The kidneys control your blood pressure. So, the kidneys are making the*

> **The med student even said today that a higher being must have been helping out on this one.**

*high blood pressure that in turn makes her heart work harder, thickening the wall and enlarging the heart. The renal arteries also look a little smaller than they should be.*

*Have I confused anyone?*

*This is at least their best guess at this point. They do not know yet if this is something she was born with and became worse as she tried to grow, if there is something blocking this part of the aorta, or if there is something around the aorta squeezing it.*

*This condition is uncommon and is super rare in a child Ella's age. Depending on the situation, the hope is that it can be corrected by surgery, or maybe even a less invasive balloon procedure. More tests will need to be completed. Not sure if they will need to treat with meds for now then surgery when she gets older or if they can correct now. Looks like the plan of attack for now is to do an angiogram (probably Thursday), then the doc said the cardiology team, renal team, and surgical team will meet Friday to discuss a game plan.*

*Dr. Darragh came by this afternoon and did a further echo of the area and showed us what exactly was going on and explained his thoughts and that they still have some things to figure out. He has been so kind from the first time we met him.*

**God is providing the doctors with wisdom.**

*We are beyond happy they found the source and have something to work toward to fix it. God is providing the doctors with wisdom. He is hearing our prayers and I believe will continue to work in Ella. Seeing on the echo what such a small defect in the body can do is unbelievable. The body is an amazing thing!*

*More uplifting news from the heart echo yesterday—her ejection fraction (the % at which the heart is pumping) has improved to about 36%!! So, she has gone from 14% to 36%. Still has a ways to go, but we will take what we can get. The heart is still enlarged, but at least it is getting stronger. It has been a big day. Hopefully, we will know some more in a couple of days. Keep up the prayers. They are making a difference! Love to all, Angela*

Emotions overwhelmed me—mixed emotions. The tears flowed down my face as I leaned into Joe. We were so hopeful they could fix the problem. As I gazed at Ella, thoughts were creeping in my mind. *How did this happen? Why did it happen? Did I do something wrong while pregnant with her? Did I cause this?* These personal fears started to haunt my mind, and I kept them to myself.

The doctor's next step would be to explore further internally. An angiogram would need to be performed. There was a glimmer of light and hope that once they were able to get a better look, maybe it was just a weird narrowing and not an obstruction. Maybe they could just balloon the narrowed part open to the correct width. Lots of optimistic thoughts were now going through my mind. I was trying to air up my balloon with hope. Even though we had only been in the hospital for seventeen days, it had already seemed like a whole new lifetime.

**Thursday, August 17, 2006, 6:14 p.m.**
**Journal entry by Joe**

*The angiogram procedure was performed today. They confirmed a narrowed section of Ella's aorta. It was a bit longer then they initially thought…about 1.5 to 2 centimeters. I know what you're thinking, how much is that?!?! Same thing we asked Dr. Hoyer. Well 2.5 cm is an inch. There were a couple other concerns that they found. The narrowed section is pretty much located at the spot where her renal (kidney) arteries branch off, kind of like a "T." Those arteries supply blood to the kidneys. Her right side artery has some abnormalities to it but is supplying blood pretty well. The left side artery is a different story. Long story short here, since her kidneys have not been receiving sufficient blood supply because of the narrowed section, the left kidney has been finding blood elsewhere. Other little veins have been forming to the kidney in order to meet blood demand. The left side artery is being described as being like a "stump," not really doing its job in supplying blood.*

*Dr. Hoyer shared with us that this is a very rare condition, with the narrowing being so close to the renal artery area. So rare that her cardiologist has seen only one case of it himself in his more than twenty years of cardiology.*

*Can it be fixed? What are the long-term effects? How did it happen? These questions are being asked and researched. Since this is such a rare thing, the doctors are gathering as much knowledge as possible from other specialists and case studies.*

*It's been a disappointing day in the fact that we were hoping for better news, like a quick fix for our baby girl. This has been the first time of actually looking at the problem. Here is the upside of things. I'm going to play the role of "half glass" since Angela's taking a break from it. Ella is still in stable condition. Her blood pressure is being stabilized, and her heart is getting better…from the standpoint of pumping more blood. Time is something we have right now. At least she is not in a critical stage where they have to perform an emergency procedure. The doctors can take a little bit of time to consult and discuss what can be done. We continue to receive the best of support from all of you. Please continue to keep us in your talks with God. Is our faith being tested? You bet it is.*

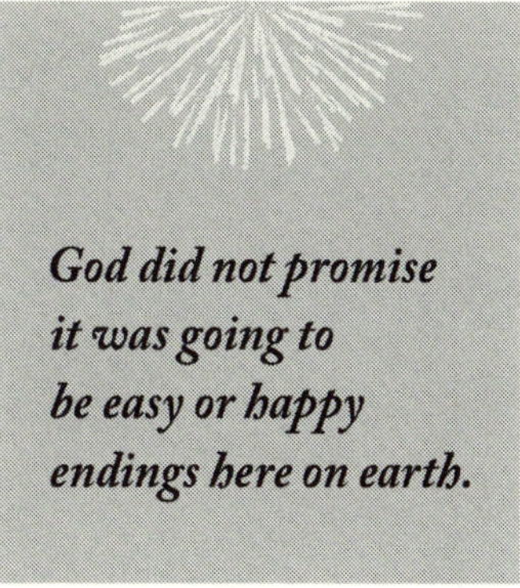


*God did not promise it was going to be easy or happy endings here on earth. What He did promise is that He would be there until the absolute end.*

*Ella continues to have her glows on the outside. The medical folks have asked, and some repeatedly, about Ella having symptoms up to this point. She really hasn't other than not gaining in size. God is working in her…and He continues to work in us.*

*Thanks again to everyone who has provided prayers and support. You have no idea how much they mean. Love to all, Joe*

**Angela's Personal Journal**

*Today was a big day. I am nervous for you.*

*Not as great of news as we had hoped for. I am pretty down. The location of the narrowing and the length with the renal arteries all make this very rare. The doctors need to figure out what to do. I feel they are worried about losing all kidney function. I was so hopeful that they would be able to go in there today and just open up the narrowed part and we could be on our merry way. I guess we don't always get exactly what we ask for. Sometimes the valley is a little longer than we would like.*

*You act so well for all that is going on inside you. You amaze me. You are so brave and strong and are so little. You don't even know how many lives you have touched.*

It's crazy to me all that we learned in such a short amount of time—medical terms and the names of body parts that you really don't think about until you need to know the names. To realize that every little fiber and part of our bodies was designed to work perfectly all together was mind blowing! How could such a small defect throw everything else off? A small narrowing in the body makes it work harder to try to correct itself and make new vessels to a kidney to try to get the proper blood flow to it. Ella's little body was doing all it could to work together and keep her alive. That just didn't happen or poof itself out of thin air. It's how God has designed us. Why are some things allowed to happen? I don't have the answer to that and may never have that here on earth. I do trust that we all will be whole in heaven and be given all the answers. I do feel that God was trying to completely open our eyes to Him and reaching others through it.

**"You are not alone"—Kari Jobe**

# Chapter 15

# GOING HOME?

**Angela's Personal Journal**

*Well, they are telling us you can go home. Even though the problem isn't fixed yet, you are stable enough with the blood pressure medicines they have you on. The doctors need time to consult, research, and decide how best to fix everything. How best to heal your heart and preserve kidney function. They don't want to keep you here if you can enjoy your time at home until they find a solution.*

*I want to go home, but at the same time, I am just nervous about being in charge of everything. One medicine you take is every four hours around the clock. They are being more lenient on how often to check your blood pressure. Since they were not able to get a portable machine for someone your size, they think once a day will be okay versus the three times a day they originally wanted. The doctor's office will check it three times a week, and Cindy will help on her off days. So thankful she is our neighbor. It would be so much crazier if we didn't have her available. We will be busy when we get home. It all seems a bit overwhelming at the moment.*

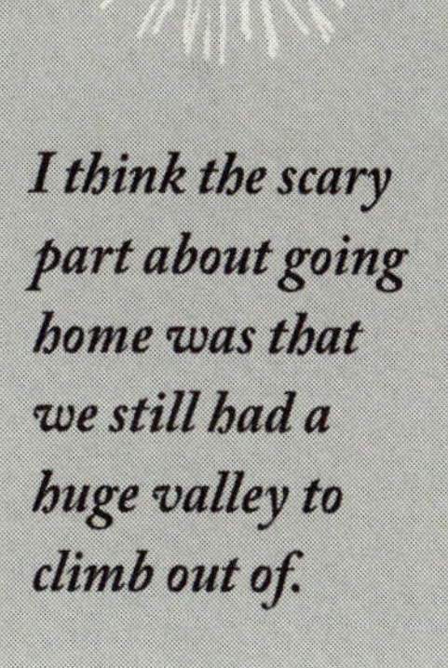

**I think the scary part about going home was that we still had a huge valley to climb out of.**

I think the scary part about going home was that we still had a huge valley to climb out of. It would have been so easy to continue to stay at the hospital in the comfort of the doctors and nurses, but Ella was stable enough to go home. Her heart and blood pressure medicines were keeping everything in check. No need to spend the extra time at the hospital while we waited for a solution. The doctors had a lot of research to do on their own. It was just daunting to think of having all the pressure and responsibility of being Ella's "nurse" and caregiver, along with the mom duties with Noah and normal household duties that I hadn't had to think about for almost three weeks, but, alas, reality had to set in at some point. And I would need to try to do my best to make things seems "normal" for Noah.

It was approaching the time when Ella would be discharged and we would have enough medicine to get us by for the evening, but we needed to fill five different prescriptions, and we had to find a place that could even make her medicine. It wasn't as easy as going to a regular grocery store pharmacy. We had to call around and found that Lafayette had one family-owned pharmacy that could make her special medicines. We were lucky enough to get a hold of them and fax over the information so the prescriptions could be picked up the next morning. That was a bit more stressful than I would have liked. The hospital did have an outpatient pharmacy, but it was super expensive, and we would need to find a local pharmacy that could make her medicines anyway.

I couldn't believe the time had come to go home. Alisha wheeled Ella out in the red wagon with her gifts packed around her. Ella waved goodbye to the nurses in the hallway. The ride home seemed to be a quiet one. It was weird to be outside of the hospital and leaving without a resolution to the problem. We were greeted at home by all of our loving neighbors. It was like they were crawling out the woodwork to greet us with hugs, meeting us in the driveway. I welcomed all of their hugs and all of them offering to help in any way they could. At that point, we had no idea what help would benefit us the most.

That evening was surreal. We were a family of four again, Noah being his active self and trying to play with Ella, and Ella trying to play with him. She started crawling. It was so weird to see. She hadn't really crawled before going into the hospital. She seemed so much livelier and enjoyed her time playing. We could just tell she was feeling better.

One thing Joe did to help with the transition of being home and the task of making sure Ella received all of her medicines at the correct time was to make a chart that we posted on the cupboard door. I appreciated the visual. I needed help with that daunting task. With needing some type of medicine about every three hours, I certainly didn't want to mess anything up.

It was such a pleasure tucking Noah into his bed for the night. We sat and chatted a bit, and I read him one of his favorite books, *I Love You This Much*. When he drifted off to sleep, I headed for Ella's room. I sat in the rocking chair for a few hours while Ella slept, just listening to her breathing. I was nervous about sleeping in my own bed even though I had longed for the comfort of my own mattress for a few weeks now. What if Ella woke up and needed something and I didn't hear her? We didn't have the extra comfort of alarms now to alert us if something went wrong. Joe convinced me that Ella would be okay, and I needed to get a good night's rest. I turned the volume of the baby monitor up as loud as it would go. Although I may not have missed Joe's snoring, I certainly had missed sleeping beside him.

We had an early appointment with Dr. Ho that next morning. I think he was excited to see Ella and surprised with how she was doing compared to that day on July 31. Since there wasn't a blood pressure machine at the pediatrician's office, he set us up to be able to go to the pediatric floor at the hospital for a blood pressure check on their machine, and we would keep track of the numbers. It was arranged where I could take her on Mondays, Wednesdays, and Fridays, and Cindy would check it for us on Tuesdays and Thursdays. The weekends were whatever worked best for everyone. It wasn't the easiest keeping her still for blood pressure checks, and even more challenging trying to wrangle an almost three-year-old while holding Ella still. I think there were several times I could have used some blood pressure medicines myself.

We tried to bring as much normalcy as we could to each day. It was strange how even some smells would take me right back to the hospital. Whatever brand of soap the hospital used, whenever I would get a whiff of that scent, it would take me right back to the restrooms in the hospital. I could smell something cherry, and it would remind me of her flavored medicine. Even the scent of Pampers diapers would bring tears to my eyes. It got to the point where I had to change our brand of diapers because it would just take me right back to her hospital room every time I changed her.

I tried to take the kids to some fun events, although I didn't want to overdo it for Ella. I carried around plungers of medication, always checking to see if Ella was looking okay and making sure she was eating and drinking enough. I didn't want to risk her becoming dehydrated. Trying to maintain the house, be a fun mom, a good caretaker, a loving wife, a successful direct sales business owner, and a decent friend was all taking its toll. I had friends (and acquaintances) offer to take Noah for a playdate and help with this and that. For some reason, Satan was interfering and telling me to push away the offers. I would always try to be polite and thank them greatly and explain we were doing good and handling things fine. Again, the insecurities were creeping into my head. I wasn't seeing it for what it really was. They were trying to bless us, which in turn blesses them. We are all supposed to help each other in the good and bad times. That is called unity and what God calls us to do. Satan was blinding me of this truth and pulling me down deeper into the pit. I was having a relationship with God, but

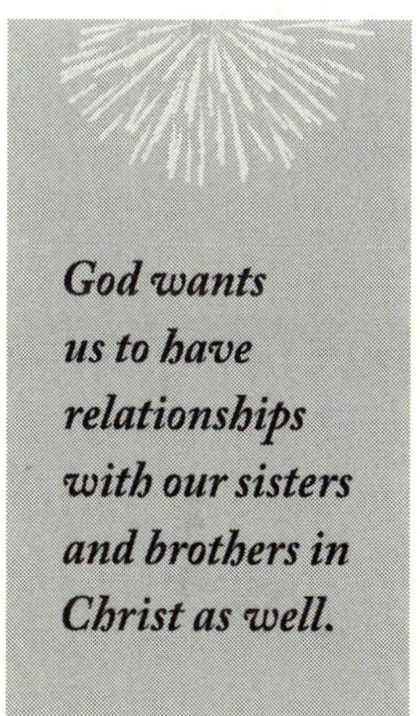

God wants us to have relationships with our sisters and brothers in Christ as well.

On the weekend before Noah's birthday, Joe's mom and dad came up for a visit. They felt comfortable watching the kids so Joe and I could have a little bit of time and prepare for Noah's birthday. The little guy was turning three, and he had been through quite the whirlwind over the last month.

We were able to celebrate Noah's birthday at Chuck E. Cheese. He had such a fun day. He enjoyed riding the little rides and playing the games to collect the tickets. Skeeball was a favorite. He would giggle when he threw the ball down the lane and always had a surprised look on his face when the ball disappeared into one the shoots at the other end. He loved seeing that crazy big grey mouse dance around, spreading the love of tickets. Ella, on the other hand, was not a fan of any kind of oversized live stuffed animal. As we cashed in our tickets at the end of our time for some "goodies" that I'm sure only lasted another day or two, we all enjoyed lots of laughter and togetherness—a nice break from what our new lives looked like.

An encouraging letter I received once home from a long-time friend gave a boost of encouragement as she knew what it was like to go through a medical trial with a child. Some of the things that rang true were,

> *"I want to tell you, you should not feel guilty about asking the 'why?' It is only natural and we need to trust that the Lord knows where our heart is when we ask it. I've been there myself with the 'why' thing,*

*and I can tell you that over time, God has led me to many different answers to that question. Answers, I may add, which I am very content with. I am hoping to offer you some sort of comfort by sharing some of them with you. I look at my life now and can't imagine it any other way. It's hard for me to see Audrey and imagine her hearing and talking. When I watch her communicate facial expressions and hand movements, they are all beautiful as if she were just born that way. I'm not saying that I don't long to hear her speak to me, but when I get to dwelling on it, all I have to do is look at her to bring myself out of it. Also, Audrey has brought so many people to us that we would not have otherwise met. People who have enhanced our lives so much that I can't imagine not knowing them now. I will pray that over time God will lead you to your own answers about Ella. Love, Amanda"*

**God will always be there for you.**

# Chapter 16

# WE HAVE A PLAN

Over the next few weeks, we continued checking Ella's blood pressure, getting further blood tests, repeating exams, adjusting her medicines. Now that she was more active at home, her blood pressure was increasing, so they needed to adjust her medications accordingly.

Another kidney scan revealed that her left kidney was continuing to lose function, almost to the point of no return. With the new information, I think a greater sense of urgency came over the doctors and surgery would have to happen sooner than later. They just needed to come to a conclusion of the best procedure.

We would meet with the surgeon, Dr. Brown, soon to gather all of his thoughts and information. Advice was given to even seek a second opin-ion. We certainly wanted the best person for the job in this unique situation. Dr. Ho recommended a second opinion with a surgeon at the Children's Hospital in Chicago. My Aunt Connie who lives in Texas actually found some information on a somewhat

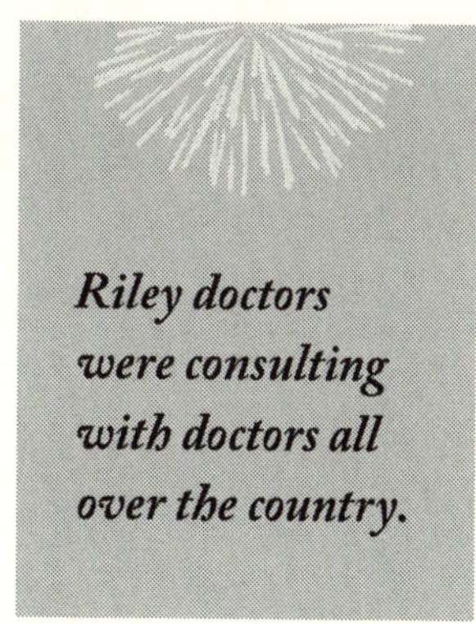

similar case at the Texas Children's Hospital. Not that we wanted to doubt the great minds at Riley, but when it is your child's life you want all the opinions that people have to offer and share. Riley certainly didn't mind us seeking other opinions. In fact, come to find out, the Riley doctors were consulting with doctors all over the country to come up with the right plan for Ella.

**Wednesday, September 27, 2006, 10:56 a.m.**
**Journal entry by Angela**

*Good morning all! Took Ella over on Monday for her blood pressure and weight check. She is over 19 lbs now! Yay! Spoke with Dr. Ho and he did a quick exam on her. He has been so wonderful and supportive through everything. We have really appreciated all his help and advice. He wanted to make sure that the Chicago hospital had contacted us to set up the second opinion, which they have. I've heard from both Texas and Chicago that they received all the info from Riley. Now just waiting to speak with the surgeons.*

*Yesterday we had a very long day. Ella had another echo-cardiogram. They gave her a sucker to try to keep her still. The sucker was everywhere and on everyone. Pretty funny! Bubbles seem to work also. The nurse would blow them right above Ella's head and she would just gaze at them as they fell all around her. Dr. Darragh didn't give any specific percentages but stated that her ejection fraction was a little better than the last echocardiogram.*

*Exciting news regarding surgery. We were able to see Dr. Brown, and he was very encouraging with the procedure they would like to do. He stated Ella is the talk of the department and the medical community. Dr. Brown has done two or three surgeries similar to this in his twenty-eight years of being a surgeon, although not in the same location as Ella's. It is riskier because of how small she is, but he was very optimistic. They want to add a patch to the aorta to make it bigger and do the same to the right renal (kidney) artery. They are unsure why the left renal artery is closed off, so they will try to flush it first and it that does not work then they will do a renal by-pass by putting in a graft (tube) for proper blood flow. There is a risk of reduced renal function while doing the procedure, but the chances are low. They still don't know why this happened and will send tissue off to pathology. Dr. Brown stated he has not heard of this procedure being done on someone so young, so only time will tell if a second surgery will be needed as she grows older. So, unfortunately, there will be periodic testing for who knows how many years. Being her mother, of course, I would love the one-time fix and just go on our merry way, but we will deal with each circumstance as it comes. We are beyond thankful that they feel they have a safe plan that will help Ella survive and thrive. They are working on getting a surgery date set for mid-October.*

*Dr. Brown knows we are getting second opinions and thought it was a good idea. I asked, "What if there are differences in opinions? Would the surgeons talk to each other?" He stated they could if needed. He can't guarantee that they would totally agree. It could possibly come down to us making the final decision. So, I am asking for prayers that the surgeons do agree so we are not put in the middle of that kind of decision for Ella.*

*We received an email from Riley, and they would like to publish Ella's story on their website. I thought that was pretty neat. I am hoping her story can give someone hope if they are dealing with a huge trial and scared for the outcome of their child. Keep the hope everyone, Angela*

❧

Later that week, we spoke with both the surgeon from Chicago and the surgeon from Texas. Chicago completely agreed with Dr. Brown's thoughts on the procedure. He had not performed this type of surgery before but put his full trust in Dr. Brown. The Texas doctor had a difference in surgical opinion. He would completely bypass the narrowed area instead of making it larger. He had done one surgery like this before, but not on someone as small as Ella. So, we would be back to the same question as to how long it would last and whether further surgeries would be needed in the future. We shared all of our information with Dr. Brown so he could discuss further with his colleagues. When it came down to it, he still felt their original surgery option was the best for Ella. We prayed about it and felt that God had us right where we needed to be. So, with a leap of faith and trusting the Lord, we decided to move forward with Dr. Brown and stay at Riley.

*So, with a leap of faith and trusting the Lord, we decided to move forward with Dr. Brown and stay at Riley.*

A few days later, we received a call from Riley that they could move Ella's surgery date up a day so that Dr. Rescorla (Chief of Pediatric Surgery) would be able to assist Dr. Brown (Chief of Pediatric Cardiothoracic Surgery).

Having two chiefs of surgery working on our precious girl gave us an even greater sense of comfort. Wow! The day was quickly approaching.

"Do not be anxious about anything, but in every situation, by prayer and petition, with thanksgiving, present your requests to God. And the peace of God, which transcends all understanding, will guard your hearts and your minds in Christ Jesus."

Philippians 4:6–7 (NIV)

# Chapter 17

# SURGERY DAY

Monday, October 16, 2006
**Angela's Personal Journal**

*W*oke up very nervous. I feel sick to my stomach at the thought of surgery and that you have no idea of what is about to happen. What you will be going through. I keep praying and praying for your health and that you will not be in a lot of pain. You have been doing so well and getting so strong. We can feel your muscles building. You are crawling all over, cruising the furniture, took your first step the other day, and you love riding on Noah's electric toddler sized four-wheeler. It is so cute to see. This morning was pretty busy. You were such a good girl, especially for not having anything to eat or drink. You didn't really want the nurses to examine you. You had x-rays and blood drawn. We gave you a bath when Mamaw and Papaw arrived. We all took shifts carrying you around. Different nurses came in and explained what will be happening before and after. They are describing that the incision will be in the front, vertical on your belly instead of the back like we had thought. I questioned them as Dr. Brown had explained they would go through the back muscles as that was closest to the aorta. They called and verified with him over the phone, and he and Dr. Rescorla now feel the front is the best approach to do their work. The change in plans makes me a bit nervous, but I am trusting that they didn't come to this decision lightly. Praying hard for you.

We thought we would see Dr. Brown, but it didn't happen as he was finishing up another surgery right before Ella's. We had to trust he knew what he was doing. He would come to see us after the surgery. As time was nearing, we gathered around Ella. With Joe holding her tightly, we joined hands, and, with nervous minds, we prayed for safety and a quick recovery. Shortly after, a nurse entered the room and gave Ella some loopy medicine to relax her as I think she could sense the tension rising. It was quite a sight. As it relaxed her, she acted like someone had spiked her bottle, laughing at the littlest of things. At about 1:15 p.m., they came to take her away to the oper-ating room. It was so hard to give her over to the nurse. As the nurse held Ella, we tucked her blankie all around her, letting the nurse know what a comfort the blan-ket was to Ella. Luckily, she went willingly. That loopy medicine did the trick. On their way out of the room, Ella looked back with her cute little grin. We all waved at her and blew kisses.

We love that little girl with all of our hearts. Roy and Connie, Mom and Skip, Chris (my step-brother), and Stacie were all at the hospital with us for support. We were instructed to go to the second floor waiting area. The nurse there would give us further instructions. Since Joe and I hadn't eaten yet for the day, we ran by the cafeteria on the first floor and grabbed some food to go. I really didn't have an appetite but knew I needed to eat a little something to keep me going. Once we arrived on the second floor, we saw a nurse sitting at a desk. We gave her our names and Ella's information. She gave Joe and me each a sticker to wear with Ella's name on it and advised us to sit wherever we felt comfortable. A surgical nurse would come by every hour with an update on how Ella was doing. We gathered some chairs around and made a little huddle. There were a few other groups of families in their own little huddles. We couldn't help but wonder what their circumstances were and hope they had good outcomes with their children.

Once we were able to sit for a few minutes, we were able to slightly exhale. Things were underway, and we were trusting the Lord's hand in all of it. Joe and I were so thankful for the company. Our conversations were proving to be a good distraction, even though I kept checking my watch for the time and wondering how long it would be before the nurse would come around and give us an update.

At 3:15 p.m., I saw a nurse enter the second floor with a clipboard. She approached each family and had a short conversation. This was it. What we had been waiting for. An update. I felt that any news was good news. The nurse came over and looked at the sticker on our shirts, then at her clipboard. With a smile on her face she told us that at 3:00 p.m. they were just getting ready to start the surgery. An IV and arterial line were in place in the left wrist, and a line in the leg. She added that Ella was doing great and wondered if we had any questions. We didn't at that point. It did seem like it took a long time for the surgery to begin. I'm sure there was so much to prepare for before the actual surgery began that we just didn't know about. We thanked her for the update, and she told us she would be back in an hour with another update.

4:15 p.m. rolled around and the nurse appeared again. Things were still going great. Dr. Brown was at the abdominal aorta and getting ready to do the patch that would open up the narrowed area. We appreciated the update. My heart started beating faster at this moment just thinking about what was going on in that operating room. I could never be a surgeon. I couldn't imagine doing the things that they do to save the lives of little ones. It blows my mind. I'm so thankful for their gifts.

We made a few calls and updated a few friends and loved ones who couldn't be there with us and at 5:05 p.m. the nurse rounded the corner with another update. She said that Ella was still doing good. Her blood pressure was a little low, but they were not overly concerned. The doctor was now working on the right renal artery. She said they cut out the irregular portion and were adding a patch to the narrowed area. She said they were very busy and didn't really have time to give a full update. As she walked off to update the next family, I grabbed my journal and started jotting the information down. This allowed me to process and keep track of the information.

The nurse appeared again at 6:05 p.m. This time was a little different though. Her demeanor still seemed chipper, but she didn't have specific details on how Ella was doing like the previous times. This, of course, concerned us a bit. She told us they were still busy, but the repair work was done, and her blood pressure was up a little. They were still monitoring closely. She added that the surgeon was making sure there were no bleeders before closing. Hopefully, the surgeon would be speaking with us shortly. Wow! It was hard to imagine that the surgery could be complete. Our family was so great. They continued to encourage us that all would be okay.

The desk nurse received a call, then came over to us to let us know that Dr. Brown would be ready soon to see us. She escorted us back to one of the surgery preparation rooms, and we waited for about twenty minutes before Dr. Brown pulled the curtain aside and greeted us. He started by saying, "The surgery went great!" A huge wave of relief ran over our bodies. I just wanted to melt into a puddle of tears. He added that Ella was doing well. He explained that he was able to open up the narrowed areas of the abdominal aorta and the right renal artery. There was tissue build up in the aorta, but they were able to clean it out. He further explained that he implanted a graft for blood flow to the left renal artery. He didn't have an answer as to why this happened to Ella but felt that this was something that just didn't develop completely as Ella was growing in my belly. Birth defects happen all the time, and this one just didn't show itself until Ella couldn't grow any longer with it. They did send off tissue to be examined. He told us the next few days would show if everything was flowing properly, and she would be monitored very closely.

We couldn't thank him enough for the amazing work that he and his staff had done. Dr. Brown told us that once Ella was out of recovery and settled into her room on the

Pediatric Intensive Care Unit, a nurse would take us to see her. Once he left the room, Joe and I stood there in a tight embrace thanking the Lord for His guidance over all that had transpired. I knew in my heart that she had been taken care of. Sometimes it's challenging to get our heads on the same page as our hearts.

We went back to the large waiting area where our family was anxiously waiting our return. We updated everyone, and it was overwhelming to see the joyous looks on their faces. Hugs were given all around. We packed up our belongings and headed to the waiting room just down the hall from the PICU. Now that Ella was out of surgery resting and would be asleep for the rest of the night, our family left for their own homes with plans to return in a day or two to visit. I still felt numb from the events of the day, and we yearned to see Ella for ourselves.

About an hour later, a nurse appeared in the doorway and motioned to us. The moment we had been waiting for all day. She was so sweet in giving us an update as we walked down the quiet hallway. As we approached the room, a knot grew bigger and bigger in my stomach. She stated that Ella was given three units of blood in transfusions, which is a lot for her size. She added, "That is about two and half times her blood volume." Again, not being in the medical field, we didn't quite understand the magnitude of that. The nurse warned us that she would look very pale, but not to be alarmed. Ella was on a ventilator and sedated so she would rest through the night. It was after 8:00 p.m. at this point when we were finally able to cross through that doorway. There was only a small light on in the room. Ella was lying there so motionless and as pale as a china doll. I think if you would have put a piece of white paper next to her face, the paper would have been a shade darker. It was so hard to see the ventilator coming out of her mouth, breathing for her. She was so cool to the touch. We stood there for several minutes, just gazing at her.

As her night nurse entered the room to introduce herself and check on Ella, she told us that in her twenty years of working at Riley, Ella was the first patient that she knew to have had this kind of surgery. She was thrilled that Ella was doing so well post-operation. We were, too! Ella's blood pressure was reading in the 70s and 80s on the monitor. Words could not express how incredible it was to see those low numbers.

Earlier in the day, Joe put our names in the drawing for a room at the Ronald McDonald House located in the hospital. We were one of the lucky ones chosen, even though I couldn't wrap my mind around leaving Ella for the evening. I knew she wouldn't be waking up, but I just didn't want to leave her side. Joe convinced me that we both needed a good night's sleep and that she would be perfectly fine overnight. He was absolutely right. As we relived the events of the day and thanked the Lord that Ella made it through the surgery safely, we were finally able to drift off to sleep in the super cushy Sleep Number bed.

"REJOICE IN THE LORD
ALWAYS. I WILL SAY IT
AGAIN: REJOICE!"

PHILIPPIANS 4:4 (NIV)

# Chapter 18

# BREATHING TUBE SCARE

We were able to get that much-needed sleep but woke up early as we were anxious to get back upstairs. We quickly packed up our things and headed for Ella's room. As we entered, it seemed brighter than the night before. It was a beautiful fall morning, and it was nice to let the warmth of the sun glow through the venetian blinds. She still looked peaceful. We sat by her side and just listened to the monitors beep and check her progress.

About mid-morning, we noticed Ella's eyes start to flutter. She was starting to wake up. This alarmed us as we didn't think she would be waking up with being on the ventilator. Her beautiful blue eyes opened, and within seconds, a look of shear fear came over her face. She was starting to panic over the vent tube down her throat. With the panicking, her blood pressure was rising, and her oxygen was going down as she was clamping down on the tube and it was

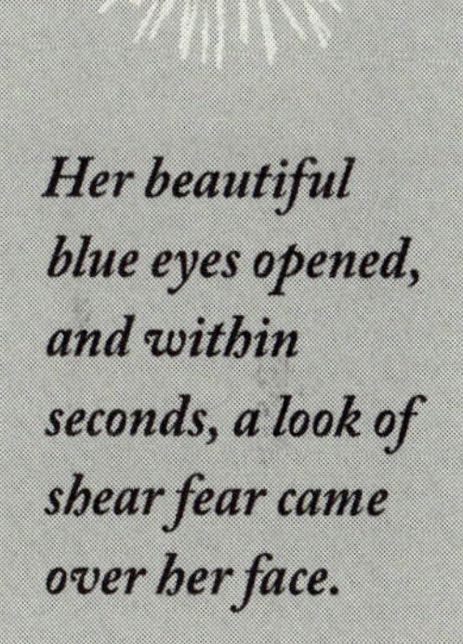

*Her beautiful blue eyes opened, and within seconds, a look of shear fear came over her face.*

not able to breath for her. I ran out of the room and looked desperately for a nurse, hollering, "She is awake. She is awake! We need our nurse!" Our nurse quickly came into the room as all the alarms were sounding.

I will never forget that terrified look on Ella's face. It still haunts me to this day. The nurse used her trusty key to open up the cart that held the sedation medicines. She quickly administered the medicine and before we knew it, the alarms quieted down and Ella's eyes were closed again. We were in shock at what had happened. The nurse said that the sedation had just worn off, and they would need to keep an eye on it to make sure she stayed asleep.

It took a while before the rush of the events settled in our own bodies. Witnessing Ella go through that shook me to the core. The sweet thing just went through major surgery and her body needed to rest as much as possible to heal. We never wanted to witness that again, and I felt one of us needed to be with her at all times, in case a nurse was urgently needed.

We had visitors throughout the day, and they allowed a few people in at a time. Roy and Connie talked us into going out to get something to eat. I was very hesitant in leaving, especially with what we had experienced just a few hours earlier. They reassured us that all would be okay, and they would sit with Ella. They knew some fresh air and some food would be good for Joe and me both.

We walked down the block and across the street to a strip mall of restaurants. Joe and I each wanted something different. I was just interested in a sandwich, and Joe was craving Chinese. I wasn't a huge fan of Chinese food at the time, so we compromised, and I got a sandwich to go and ate it in the Chinese restaurant with Joe. We always make things interesting. We tried to chit-chat and have some conversation other than the hospital, but nothing else was really coming to our minds. We enjoyed the crisp fall air and sunshine on the walk back. The brief break was lovely, but we both wanted to get back to be by Ella's side.

As we entered the room, we could see that Roy looked pretty distraught. We eagerly asked him what had happened. Ella had woken up again. And again, the alarms went off and the nurse had to rush in and give Ella medicine to sedate her. Poor Roy was in there by himself as Connie had stepped out to use the restroom. Roy said he was so scared and never wanted to see anything like that again. I felt so bad for him as he described the experience with tears in his eyes. Witnessing it, we knew the panic that it stirred in our bodies. To see such fear on a baby girl's face just breaks one's heart. We hugged him and Connie and apologized up and down that they had to see that. I am sure that it struck a nerve and brought him back to a time with his own daughter, Sheryl. Some things can never truly escape your mind.

*To see such fear on a baby girl's face just breaks one's heart.*

Thankfully, Ella was resting well again and snuggled up in her blankie, lying there peacefully once again. And we were praying that would be the last breathing tube scare.

We were greeted late afternoon by Dr. Brown. He was pleased with Ella's numbers but was not happy that she was waking up out of her sedation. So he changed her medicine to keep her more relaxed. Fingers crossed, the tube would be coming out tomorrow.

I stayed in the room with Ella that night. A nurse brought a recliner into the room so I would have a place to sleep. After the events of the day, I was not going to leave Ella's side. I was looking forward to a new day and praying for good news.

**Angela's Personal Journal**

*Praying over you tonight. Praying for God to wrap His loving, healing arms around you and that you will stay sedated so your little body can rest and heal. Thank you, Lord, for bringing her through the surgery.*

*CaringBridge guest post: "I pray that as time passes, you and Joe can look back on this time with peace in your heart, knowing that God always has a plan. Love, Julie"*

# Chapter 19

# WE CAN ALL BREATHE EASIER NOW

Wednesday, October 18, 2006, 11:05 a.m.
Journal entry by Angela

*Breathing tube is out! Ella is doing well, and it is so nice to get a step further on the road of recovery.*

*T*hank you, Lord, that the breathing tube has been re-moved! I think we were all breathing better now that the tube was out. Those were a couple of intense days. Ella was still lying still, but she was awake and looking around the room. We talked softly to her as she gently rubbed her little fingers over part of her blanket with one hand, and Joe smoothly rubbed the top of her other hand. As the day went on, she became more alert, but still no emotion on her face. Late in the evening, we were able to give Ella some Pedialyte. I held the bottle to her mouth as she drank two ounces right down and wanted more. We could only give two ounces at a time to make sure her tummy could handle it. We didn't want to overdo it and cause her to vomit. That would be too traumatic for her system right after surgery. Her blood pressure had crept up some, which concerned us, but the doctors reassured us it was okay and said to expect that for several months as her body healed and leveled out. What was surprising to us, though, was that it was getting a little higher when she wasn't even upset. It would rise with just the simple task of drinking her liquids.

Another post-operation task was to make sure fluid didn't build up in her lungs. A sweet nurse came around to give "pitter pats." She had a little, pink, cone-shaped tool that looked like a toy. She would tap Ella's chest and back. The thumping up and down movement would suction the skin a bit and keep things flowing and not settling on the inside. Since Ella was not mobile yet, we didn't want to risk the chance of her getting pneumonia.

The next day, Dr. Brown said Ella was stable enough to move out of the PICU. The move to the heart floor was a welcome change. We were able to see some familiar faces, and the nurses were happy to see her, too! They had been getting updates on Ella and were anxiously awaiting her arrival. We had the chance to get a better look at Ella's incision as they changed out the bandage. Sweet baby girl's incision started at the top of her belly, straight down, curved around her belly button and stopped above her pelvic area. It was going to make for quite the lengthy scar—one I hoped she would grow to own proudly as she had been through so much. Once it was covered with a fresh bandage, the nurse added a cute Winnie the Pooh sticker to the top to give it a colorful look.

*Over the next few days, her spunk started returning.*

Over the next few days, her spunk started returning. She was drinking and getting her appetite back with little sips and bites here and there. Her first word after surgery was "duck." I was reading her a little book with bright colorful animals on it. She pointed her little finger to the yellow creature and said, "Duck". It caught me off guard as I hadn't heard her say anything since surgery day. It was so good to hear her precious little voice again. I smiled at her, and she gave a tiny little grin back.

As each day passed, she became more mobile in her bed. When she was transferred back to the heart floor, she was moved to a different bed that kind of resembled a crib. The bars came up about chest high for a standing adult. For Ella, it allowed her to be able to stand up in bed and not to fall out as the top came up to about her shoulders. Wires were being removed, and she was getting some energy back. It was wonderful to see that glow in her eyes and the squish of her cheeks. Her incision was looking great, and she really didn't mind the bandages covering up her poochy belly.

She enjoyed eating in bed. One of her favorites was French toast sticks. She would stand up in bed and take a bite and then offer me a bite. She enjoyed listening to fun children's songs. I would read some CaringBridge guest posts to her. I am sure she didn't understand what I was reading, but it helped pass the time, and I certainly enjoyed the encouragement from our family and friends. One thing that was lingering in the back of my mind was that her blood pressure kept creeping up and her face would turn red and become a little sweaty with little movement. The doctors continued to adjust the medications, and they decided they had to start her back on a blood pressure medicine. That was a bit disheartening. She had been off all of the blood pressure medicines for a few days, but with the increasing pressure, they couldn't wait any longer and risk it getting too high.

We were nearing day ten of being in the hospital this round. There were talks of us going home soon. Dr. Andreoli wanted to do a renal scan to check how Ella's kidneys were functioning, and we agreed that was a great step before being released. I feared they were concerned with something post-surgery. Sometimes, it is challenging having a mother's instinct. We couldn't have been more thankful with how Ella was acting those days after surgery, but our best case scenario was not to need blood pressure medicines any longer. I had to keep reminding myself to take it one day at a time.

We were looking forward to having a visit from Noah. As we anticipated his arrival, Joe kept asking Ella where Noah was, and she would look around the room trying to find him. It was a pretty cute sight to see. Noah was enjoying his time with relatives. I think Aunt Stacie and Uncle Jim were having fun spoiling him and getting a glimpse of what it would be like as parents when their little one arrived in a few months. One story they shared was that they took Noah to lunch at McDonald's and thought it would be fun for him to be able to run around in the playland area. They ate lunch right next to the tubes and tunnels that the little kids could climb in. Noah made a little friend, and they were running back and forth. After a while, and after a few kids had passed by, Jim and

Stacie noticed an odor. They began thinking, *Some parent needs to check their kid's pants, because someone needs a change.* A little while longer, Noah passed by again, and I think the light bulb came on for both of them at the same time. It wasn't someone else's kiddo. It was the kiddo that they were in charge of. Once they were able to grab Noah, it didn't take long to confirm that it was him. Not used to the whole parenting thing yet, they hadn't brought a diaper bag or anything of use with them on their lunch adventure. So, they strapped Noah in his car seat and drove down the road with all of the windows down, trying to get home as quickly as possible. This story gave us some belly laughs, which we needed during our hospital stay.

When Noah arrived, he entered the room like he had been there a thousand times. Ella was happy to connect eyes with him. Noah had brought a special treat for Ella—a red, cherry-flavored Twizzler. He tried to feed it to her, and she was all about trying to eat that thing. We enjoyed our special time with Noah. At the end of our visit, we told him we would be home soon. Part of me was not sure if he even realized we were not at home. I really am okay with that, though. We knew he was being well taken care of, and we would rather Noah have a good time than worry about things that little boys shouldn't have to worry about.

"Rejoice always, pray without ceasing, give thanks in all circumstances; for this is the will of God in Christ Jesus for you."

1Thessalonians 5:16-18 (ESV)

# Chapter 20

# GOOD NEWS AND BAD NEWS

Thursday, October 26, 2006, 7:47 p.m.
Journal entry by Angela

*Well, we have good news and bad news. The good news is that we are home!*

*We arrived a couple of hours ago. Ella had a big testing day. Even with the loopy medicine, she was still upset during the kidney scan. Songs and books were not keeping her as calm as I had hoped.*

*Bad news of the day: the left kidney was not showing up on the screen during the scan. Those dots just didn't want to appear on that left side. The results are that the left kidney is showing little to no function at this point. The doctors are unsure if it is from the trauma of the surgery or if a possible blood clot has formed in the graft and is blocking flow to the kidney. The doctors will need to talk amongst themselves to see what the next plan of attack will be. We will have another kidney scan in a month to check for changes. Thankfully, the right kidney function was normal. Thank you, Jesus!*

*Dr. Darragh was on the heart floor today before we left and was brought up to speed. He wheeled in a machine and did an echocardiogram on her. He wanted to see for himself how she was doing. I was very thankful for that. He said her heart function looked a little better than before surgery. He wasn't seeing blood flow through the left kidney graft, which confirms what the kidney scan showed. He was going to discuss this with the other doctors and wants to see Ella back in two weeks.*

*Should they do any other type of procedure to the kidney? Or give it time to see if there is any improvement? He made it sound like if it is a blood clot, that is one of the risks involved with surgery, and it is not the perfect outcome that we were hoping for. We will just have to wait and see. She can live with one kidney. It would just mean that they would have to monitor the right one even more closely. Dr. Darragh made it sound like she would probably need more procedures as she grows to make sure that right renal artery is staying open to give proper blood flow to the right kidney.*

*My heart aches for Ella that she didn't have the perfect outcome. There really isn't perfection here on earth, though. Her medical journey isn't over yet. We are beyond thankful that she is alive and thriving. We may just have to work at it a little longer to get everything worked out. For now, we will continue to have her blood pressure checked daily, and adjust her medications as needed. God's not done with her yet.*

*Ella is acting wonderfully. She doesn't seem to be in pain. She is smiling and laughing. Her urine culture*

*came back showing no infection and less blood in it than the day before.*

*It is good to be home! I kept asking the doctors today if we were really ready, and they reassured me she could go home. We will handle things outpatient. With everything that happened today, I am still nervous for her, but I have to trust that she has the best care possible.*

*Please continue to keep her in your prayers as we still have a ways to go. I thank you with all my heart. Love, Angela*

*CaringBridge guest post: "God is so faithful. He's so good to us. May His blessings continue to just fall all over you over and over. All my love, Aunt Jeannie"*

ELLA AT ABOUT TEN MONTHS OLD

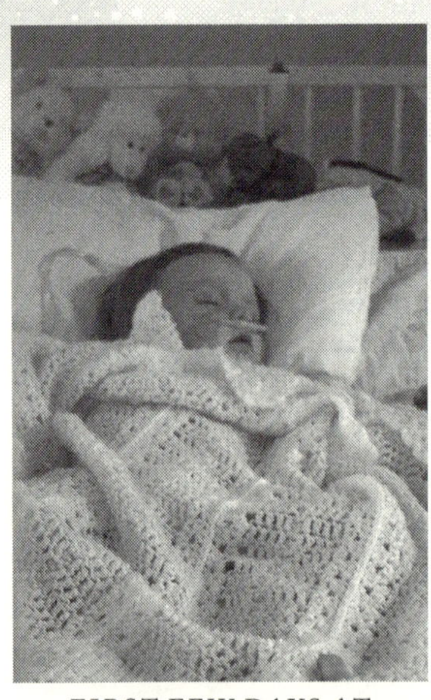

FIRST FEW DAYS AT
ST. VINCENT HOSPITAL

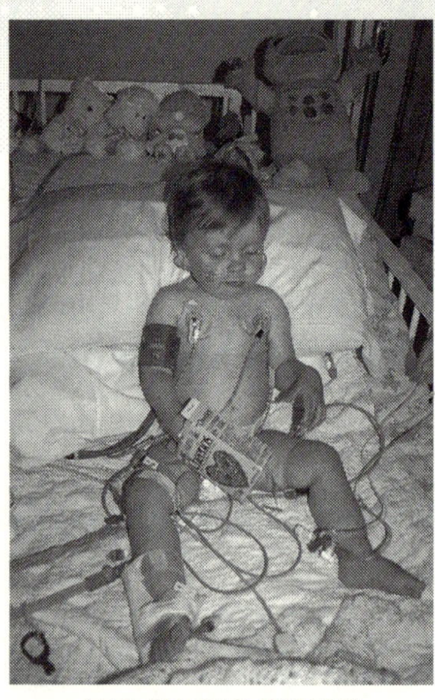

ALL THOSE WIRES

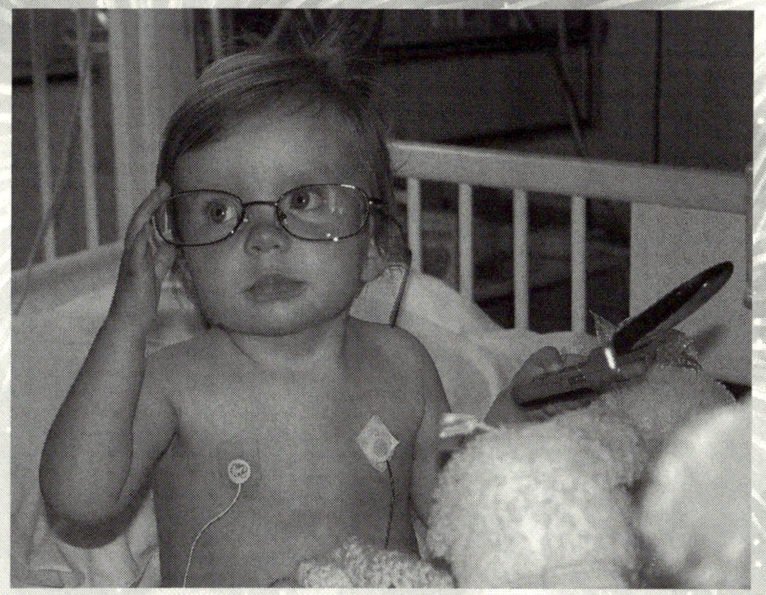



THE MOVE TO RILEY HOSPITAL FOR CHILDREN.
PLAYING WITH DADDY'S GLASSES AND
CALLING FOR HELP

A RIDE IN THE LITTLE RED WAGON

NURSE ALISHA TO THE RESCUE

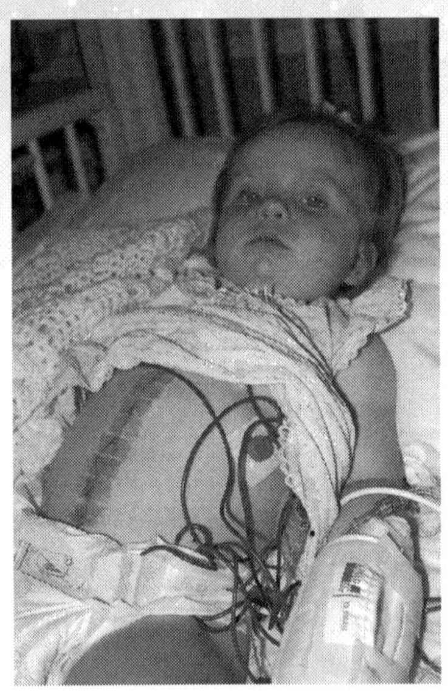

ELLA'S FIRST
MAJOR SURGERY

NOAH SHARING A
TWIZZLER WITH ELLA

MAKING A WISH

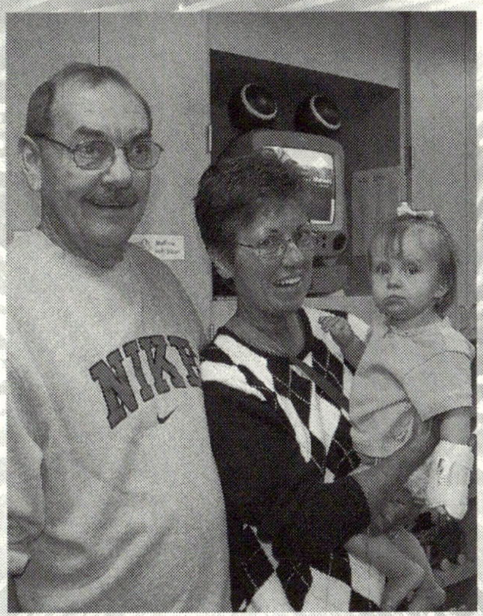

MAMAW AND PAPAW
VISITING

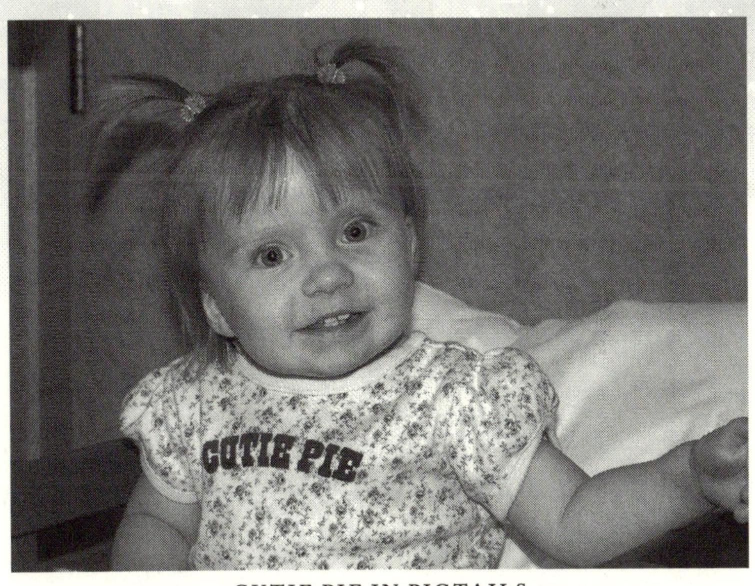

CUTIE PIE IN PIGTAILS

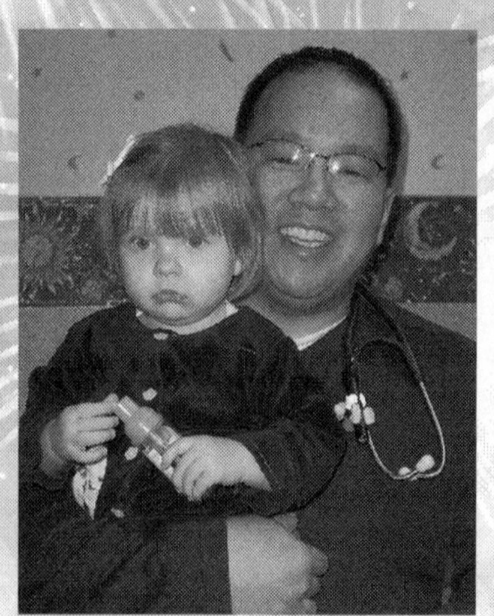

DR. HO AND ELLA

DR. ANDREOLI AND ELLA

FAMILY PICTURE IN 2008

GRANDMA AND GRANDPA
HELPING AT A
RILEY APPOINTMENT

ELLA WITH A STATUE OF JAMES WHITCOMB RILEY

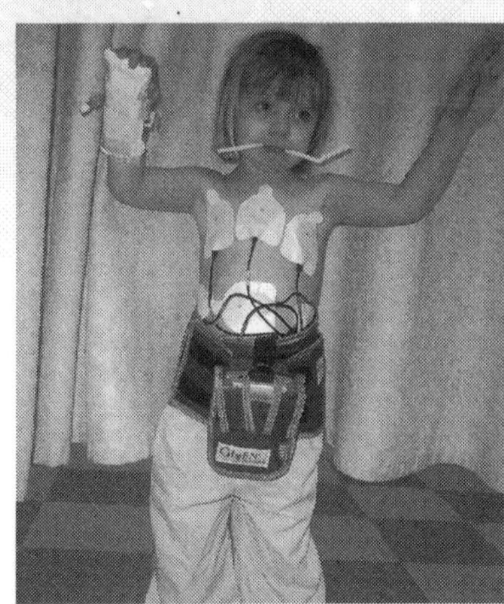

GETTING READY FOR
LIFT-OFF WITH THE
PILL CAM TEST

THIS IS WHAT SHE
THINKS OF HER UPCOM-
ING PROCEDURE

DR. DARRAGH AND ELLA

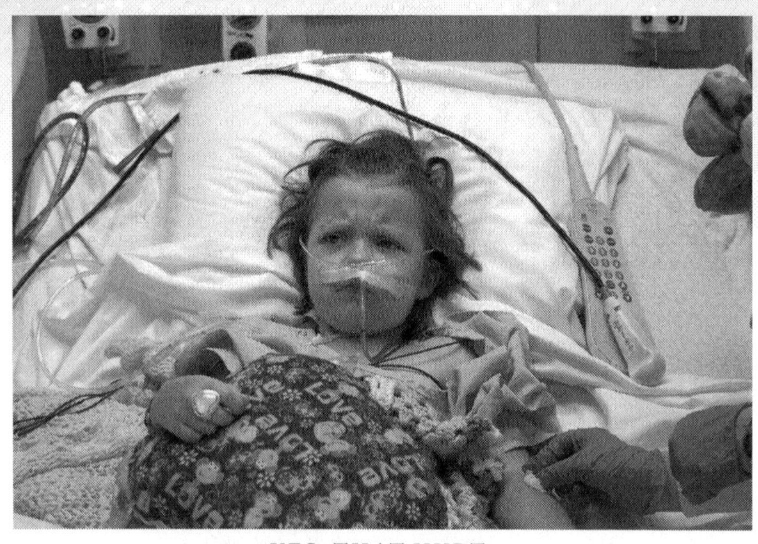

YES, THAT HURT!

WAGON RIDE WITH HER COUSINS,
SAMANTHA AND TORIE

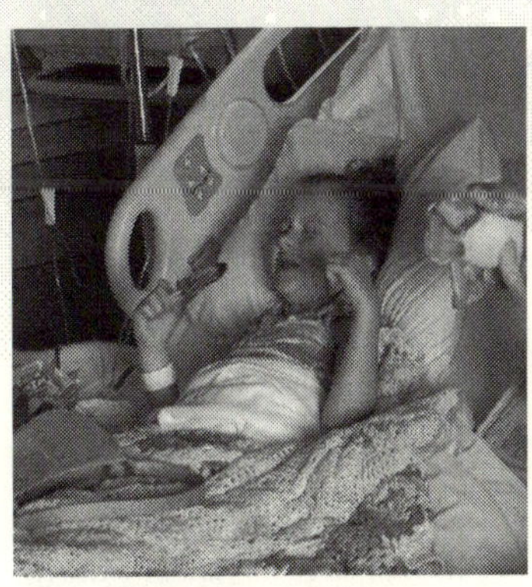

OH, THAT PURPLE
POPSICLE AND
MUSICAL CARD

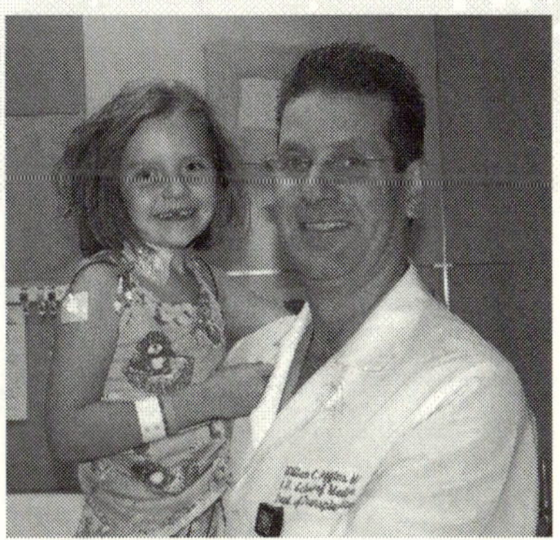

ELLA AND DR. GOGGINS

FAMILY PICTURE IN 2015

VOLUNTEERING AT GIVE KIDS THE WORLD IN 2017

LAST VISIT WITH DR. ANDREOLI BEFORE
SHE RETIRED FROM HER PRACTICE

2020 FAMILY PICTURE

# Chapter 21

# CHURCH FAMILY

Over the next several days of getting settled at home, we were blessed by several people bringing us meals. It's the little things that make such a huge difference. An acquaintance at the time, Krystal, had shared with her church members about our family, and they jumped on board to bless us with meals. Although this act seemed somewhat simple, it had a huge impact on us. At first, Joe thought it was a bit strange. Why would we need people that we didn't know bring us meals when we could cook for ourselves? Joe didn't realize at the time that I needed all the extra help I could get as I was struggling more internally than I would let on.

We were just so wowed by this act of kindness as the church that we had attended somewhat regularly barely reached out to see how we were doing. We knew the Lord and loved the Lord, but it wasn't until we met the people at Elston that we knew truly what church community was about.

Joe didn't grow up attending church regularly. He knew about God and believed there was a God but didn't really know about salvation and being God-centered. I didn't start attending church until I was almost a teenager, when the new pastor and his family moved in right across the street. Mom and the pastor's wife became friends, and we started attending church with them.

When Joe and I moved to Illinois, right out of college, we sought out a church to attend together and ended up at a mega church. We helped serve and were part of a family group. I think we were doing the right things, but I don't think Joe had truly let the Lord capture his heart. When we moved back to Indiana, it was a struggle to get connected to a new church. The feeling wasn't the same, and it became harder when we had an infant who didn't do well in the nursery. Thankfully, that all changed when we found the small, family-loving, dirt-digging, deal-with-your-crap-and-heal-from-it, God-needs-to-be-in-the-center-of-your-marriage church at Elston Family Church. God's timing is always good, and He knew what we needed during this time in our lives.

In the spring of 2007, we were invited to a spaghetti dinner hosted by Elston, which I drug Joe along to a bit reluctantly. We needed this time as a couple and to meet other couples. We were seated at a table with a wonderful young couple who also had two small children. We felt this instant connection as well with a few other people there that night. We exchanged stories and laughter. It was such a refreshing night. I was starting to get this sense that God was placing these people in our lives for a reason.

The next thing I knew, Carrie, my friend and neighbor, and I were going to a women's retreat with the ladies from Elston. It truly was a turning point in my faith and the road that I was on. I was first introduced to the songs by Christian artist Kari Jobe. What an angelic voice she has. One of the speakers at the retreat had put together a video of her daughter along with the song "My Beloved" by Kari Jobe. The tears just started flowing down my face as the words resonated with me. I could only think of Ella and how God loves her the most. I couldn't imagine how He could love her any more than Joe and I, but she is His child first. He wanted me to cast my fears at His feet and give all my worries about Ella and Noah to Him.

That evening, there was worship time. The lights were lowered, the music was soft and lovely, everyone was standing, arms lifted high, praising the Lord. Some of the women leaders lined the front of the room, ready to pray with whomever might be in need of prayer. I so wanted to go up there but felt weird as I really didn't know these ladies. I must have had an aura around me, as I felt a gentle nudge on my shoulder. I turned around and looked at this sweet young lady who encouraged me to go up front. To not be afraid. That was my sign. I went forward and met Darla, the sweetest lady you will ever meet, short and petite but with a heart that is larger than life. She prayed over me, and we cried together. We had an immediate connection. I felt like I could just melt in her hug. The stress and weight that I had been carrying was crumbling away, and I was feeling God's loving arms wrapped around me so tightly. I was finally able to relax. The circumstances were still there, but to have a moment to breathe was priceless. A connection was made with so many women at that retreat. I was able to come home refreshed, and I was so excited to tell Joe all about it and to share about these incredible ladies.

The very next Sunday, the four of us attended church at Elston, and we felt right at home. The worship music was what we were looking for, Pastor Randy on keyboard and Lindsay on vocals with her Kari Jobe sound. The preaching was biblically-based, and the family units were right where we were. We jumped right in and started connecting. Joe connected with some wonderful, godly men who were able to help him deal with some of the demons going on in his own head. We met our best friends at Elston. Scott and Jessica had two younger kids, a boy and a girl, and such a passion for connecting and serving others. We knew God planted us there to deal with some of the toughest trials in our lives. God doesn't want us to go through life alone.

*God has put people in your life on purpose.*

# Chapter 22

# NEW THINGS
# ARE HAPPENING

Sunday, March 4, 2007, 3:26 p.m.
Journal entry by Joe

*Hello everyone. Joe here. Here on a wonderful Sunday afternoon with a few moments to catch up on things.*

*We had a chance to share Ella's Riley story over the last couple weeks. She, and we, were invited to share her testimony of how Riley Hospital for Children holds a special place in our hearts. Purdue University had their third annual Dance Marathon for Riley kids. I believe they had around 600 Purdue students who gave of themselves to help children. They raise money throughout the year, and then end it all with a big lock-in on Saturday night with a dance party. We got on the stage, and Angela read about Ella's story. A very emotional time as it is still raw. Purdue students raised over $55,000. Way to go, black and gold!*

*The following Friday, the local radio station WKOA held their first annual Riley Radio-a-thon, asking listeners to become "Miracle Makers." On live air, one of the hosting DJs asked us to share Ella's story. I said us, but I meant Angela. I kept Ella occupied. We hope sharing our story brings light to how wonderful of a hospital Riley is.*

*How's our little Angel Ella coming along? Great! Every day we watch that little miracle walking around here with the smile that God gave her. Her own personality is definitely getting stronger. She knows what she wants/likes and not. Believe me! She and Noah are starting to play more together. Noah still wants to wrestle with her a little too much, but I'm sure that won't last once Ella learns to put him into submission someday. Hehe.*

*She is walking pretty quickly wherever she seems to want to go. She is also starting to climb up on chairs and the couch. Her strength is really good, too. Let her get you with one of her grips, and you will know what I'm talking about. Her hair is getting longer, and Angela is having a fun time putting it up into pigtails and such. It does look very cute on her, I have to admit.*

*Her weekly blood pressure checks seem to be in line with all that's going on. No extra calls to the doctors have been required. From this point forward, we will be visiting Riley about every three to four months so measurements can be taken of her kidneys. She's still on the various blood pressure medicines, but she takes them very well.*

*Better get going. Love you all, Joe*

A few months later, something new started occurring with Ella. She would wake up from a dead sleep and start vomiting. We would hear her stirring through the baby monitor. It would start as a whimper, then a small cry, then the dry heaves. We would jump out of our bed and run to her room. Ella would violently vomit several times, then just fall right back to sleep. I think the effort of her vomiting wore her out. We would rock in the chair with her in our arms while she slept. About ten minutes later, the process would start over again. The poor sweet thing. This process would continue on over a two- or three-hour timespan. Once it had finally passed, she would sleep for a few hours, then wake up like nothing had happened. No fever, no achiness. She would be ready for the day. It was so strange. I took her to see Dr. Ho, but with no other symptoms, he said the best thing to do was to wait and see if it occurred again.

About four weeks later, the same thing happened, and again about another four weeks after that. One early morning, we heard her stirring through the baby monitor and knew what was coming so we rushed in her room and scooped her up. We held a little bucket in front of her, hoping to catch as much of the mess as we could. We had done a lot of laundry to this point. We learned some tips to try to ease up on the washing machine. After a few vomiting spells, I thought she was done. As she fell asleep, I laid her on the floor to change her diaper as it was pretty full at this point. While in the middle of it she started to stir and all of the sudden stuff was spewing out of her mouth and all over her face. I felt like I couldn't grab her up quick enough. I called for Joe and he ran in. Ella was crying as she had vomit all over her face and in her eyes. We hurried into the bathroom and ran cool water across her face and wiped her eyes clean. Stuff was everywhere. We were able to finally calm her down after her eyes stopped hurting. We cleaned things up the best we could and rocked her back to sleep. Joe was always good about staying calm in crazy situations. Joe sat in the chair with her, and she was able to sleep a few more hours, but her little eyes were red the rest of the day. And many times, she would have little red blotches on her face because small blood vessels would rupture from the violent vomiting.

At our next visit, I described to Dr. Andreoli what had been occurring, and she did find it strange. With Ella's odd medical history, she thought we should look into it a little further. We didn't want to take anything lightly.

*"We love to hear things are going well for Ella.*
*We continue to pray for her and your family. I enjoy being*
*able to check her update. We are here for you, anytime you*
*need help with anything! We love ya! We serve a big*
*and great God! The Milsaps Family"*

# Chapter 23

# ADDING NEW DOCTORS

I received a late afternoon call from Dr. Andreoli. She would typically call once she received Ella's blood work back from an appointment to update me on numbers. I really appreciated that she did this. This time she was calling to let me know that Ella's hemoglobin was very low, and I needed to bring her back to Riley. I was panicked as Joe was three hours away for a business trip, and I needed to find a place for Noah quickly. Mom took Noah, and I rushed Ella back down to Riley. We were instructed to go to the emergency room, and there she would be admitted. Things don't always go as smoothly as we would like. The ER nurse didn't quite get the full memo as to why we were there. Once everything was figured out, Ella was admitted and more bloodwork was done. Joe was able to cut his work trip short and headed home to be with us.

Ella's numbers had dipped below 8, which was usually when they would give a blood transfusion, but they decided to first give her some iron supplements to see if that would boost it a bit. The plan was to monitor overnight. Dr. Andreoli introduced us to one of Riley's hematologists.

Ella had to be losing blood from somewhere. It just didn't add up that all of the sudden she would be anemic. *A new piece to Ella's puzzle.* The doctors weren't sure if her loss of iron in her blood was related to her vomiting or something totally separate.

With her being more aware of things, we had to be a little more creative during testing and getting her to do the things we needed her to do. She got to go poopy in a "hat" on the potty. The "hat" was a plastic winged bucket that would sit in between the seat and the bowl to collect urine or stool samples. Sitting on the potty to do her business into something where it didn't flush away was a new concept. Once we had a sample, the nurse swabbed it, and it came back positive for blood.

The pressure started to rise again within me. We had been on a decent path and now new things were starting to arise in Ella's body. Somehow and from somewhere, she was losing blood, and it was coming out in her stool, making her anemic. We already had a scheduled appointment to see a gastroenterologist at Riley, but with this new finding, everything seemed to be moving at a faster rate.

After a few days in the hospital, Ella's iron numbers increased to the point where we could go home. We added an iron supplement to the list of daily medicines. Ella was not at the point that she would swallow a pill, so it was a liquid iron medicine. If you have never had to take an iron supplement before, count yourself lucky, especially if it is a liquid form. Trust me, it smells and tastes just like iron. It would be like licking an iron pole up and down for about five minutes. Even though our local pharmacy flavored it the best they could, it would still leave a nasty aftertaste, and after the first time of Ella taking that medicine, the battle was on. She began refusing to take any of her medicines. She thought everything was going to taste as nasty as the iron medicine. We would try to disguise it. Switch from juice to medicine. We could get by with it for a short amount of

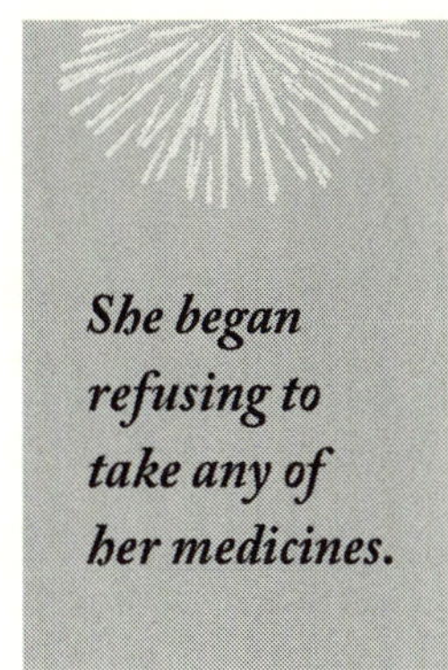

*She began refusing to take any of her medicines.*

time, but it got to the point where we had to hold her and squeeze her little checks so her mouth would open and squirt the medicine in as far back as we could get it so she wouldn't spit it back out. This was occurring multiple times a day and not the battle I wanted to fight with my precious girl.

We added a hematologist and a gastro doctor to our rotation of doctors to see. The gastro doctor added another new medicine to hopefully help with her vomiting spells. Ella had an endoscopy, colonoscopy, and a pill camera that took pictures every few seconds to capture her middle intestines. The last test was interesting. She looked like a super hero with a utility belt strapped around her waist and big white rectangular leads stuck to her chest. Because they needed to capture so many pictures with the camera traveling through her middle intestines, the test took eight hours.

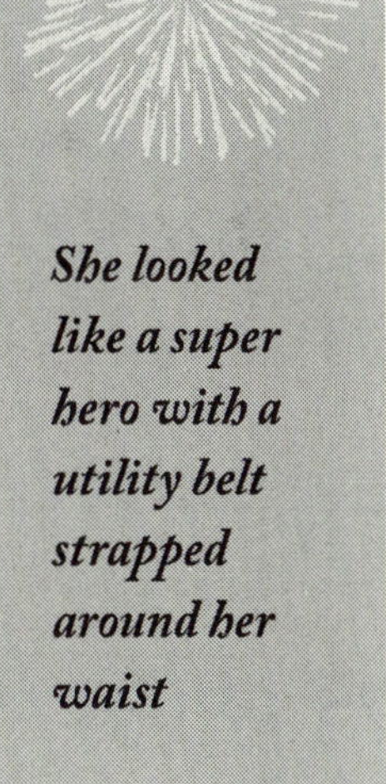

*She looked like a super hero with a utility belt strapped around her waist*

They lightly sedated her and placed the pill camera in her stomach so it would get to her intestines quicker. The blessing is that she was mobile, and she had a digital pack on that was transferring all the info to the hospital to be monitored. We were able to leave the grounds, so we went to the fabulous Children's Museum that was only a few miles away. She handled it all like a champ. And thankfully, she was starting to come around on taking her medicines—at least the ones that didn't smell like iron. At the end of the day, we returned the items back to Riley for review, except for the pill camera. That would come out on its own in a day or two. Sure enough, we were at Stacie's house when it came out, and Joe thought it would make a great souvenir.

Most days, I was either at the pharmacy, at an office checking Ella's blood pressure, taking Noah to preschool, or at a Riley appointment. There were definitely some blurry days. Ella was randomly testing positive for blood in her stool. Her iron levels were staying in a good range with the supplements, but her blood pressure was continuing to rise and so was the amount of her medicines. Another kidney ultrasound showed the narrowing getting worse in the artery that gave blood to her right kidney. We wouldn't be able to keep going down the same path. *Oh Lord, why is this happening again?* Fear was creeping back in.

**You are strong.**

# Chapter 24

# BALLOON #1

Wednesday, March 18, 2009
Journal entry by Angela

*We have another plan!*

*After a few weeks of talking with doctors and the doctors talking with each other—we have a plan of attack.*

*Ella will be having surgery tomorrow. The interventional radiologist will go through the femoral artery in her leg to the right renal artery and measure the exact size of the artery. If it does in fact look as narrow as it shows from tests, then he will do an angioplasty (balloon procedure) to widen the artery. This will help blood flow to the right kidney and hopefully will help it to be able to grow again.*

*From the last gastro test they did (the pill cam), they did see little bleeder areas in the upper intestines. He explained it like open wounds. He is unsure why they are there. This does solve why she has been losing blood and has become anemic. The hematologist was thrilled to have an answer to that. One reason for the bleeding spots could be poor blood flow in the intestine/bowel. While they are in working on the right kidney, the same doctor will be able to perform a test on the bowel/intestine to check blood flow.*

*I am at least thankful they can do it at the same time. Hopefully this test will give the doctors direction on the blood in the stool issue and we can correct it.*

*Tomorrow will be a big day! I am praying for direction for the doctors, quick healing for Ella. I am praying that Ella will continue to be a trooper through it all. I have not told her yet what she is in for. We will be heading down to my sister's house tonight to stay there. Then we need to be at the hospital at 7:30 a.m., and the surgery is scheduled at 9:00 am.*

*Ella will most likely need to stay at the hospital overnight. We will keep you posted as we can.*

*Thank you for all your prayers and support.*

*Love to all, Angela*

Joe, Ella, and I settled into the small waiting area. Of course, our hearts were pounding a bit as we were facing

another surgery. Even though this surgery couldn't compare to the last, it still was a surgery and things could still go wrong. We were about to say a prayer over the surgery when the surgeon came in to discuss the process of the procedure and asked if he could sit in on our prayer. Uh, yes! Absolutely! I love doctors of faith! We prayed, and he reassured us that all would be well.

I was able to carry Ella back to the small room where they would get her ready for surgery. It was a bright room with a long hospital bed waiting for her. She began to squirm as we were both nervous. She wasn't ready to sit on the bed, so she stood as I changed her into a flowing pale pink hospital gown, then held her as she picked out the root beer flavored Chapstick and the nurse applied it to the clear device that would fit over her nose and mouth. We told Ella to smell the yummy flavor as she breathed in the air filled with anesthetic. She was able to calm down, laid on the bed, and quickly drifted off to sleep. It was time for me to leave the room as the nurse would take it from there and prepare Ella for the procedure.

The procedure lasted less than an hour. The surgeon returned to the waiting room to inform us that Ella did great, and they were able to balloon open the artery for better blood flow. He believed it would help her blood pressure greatly! Everything else looked good. Ella was in recovery, and we could go back and see her shortly. The tricky part now was that Ella will have to lay flat and not move her leg for a few hours. *What?* That was not going to be easy with a toddler who would not understand why she couldn't move around. Luckily, she would still be under sedation for a while. We thanked him immensely for taking care of our girl.

The nurse came to our waiting area and escorted us back to Ella. She looked so peaceful lying there under the blankets that were keeping her warm. I brushed her hair to the side with my hand. She still felt cool to the touch. The kind nurse was whispering to us and reiterating how important it was for Ella to be completely still for the next few hours. With a procedure through the femoral artery, there can be a high risk of bleeding out of that major vein, so she needed to be still until that area clotted properly. As she was talking to us, she continued to lift the blanket to check the incision area to make sure all was well.

Ella started to stir a bit as she was waking up from the anesthetic. The nurse quickly checked Ella's leg and all was good. Ella started to open her eyes a bit, and we calmly held her hand. The nurse told Ella that she needed to stay completely still. She lifted the blanket to check the incision area again, and suddenly Ella was laying in a pool of blood. It seriously was a matter of seconds. The nurse went into panic mode as Ella was bleeding out from her femoral artery. She quickly put both of her hands on Ella's leg and started calling for backup. Joe and I could tell by the tone in the nurse's voice that this was serious, and there was nothing we could do. Ella had a frightened look on her face, and I shielded her eyes and just began praying over her. "Father, please lay your healing hands on Ella and stop this bleeding from happening." I just kept repeating myself over her for what felt like an eternity. But, after a few minutes the surgeon came in with such a calm demeanor. The nurse stepped aside, and he gently placed two fingers on Ella's inner thigh where they had made the incision. He calmly told the nurse that it just needed some moderate pressure to stop the bleeding and allow the clot to form. He held his fingers there for a few

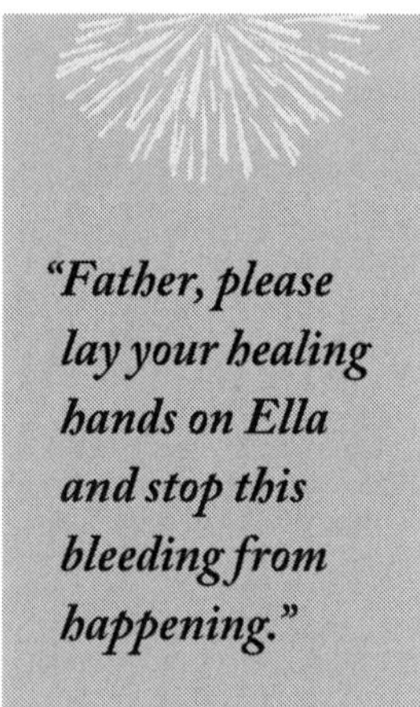

minutes, and once he removed them, all seemed well. We were able to exhale at that moment. I know the nurse was just trying to help, but her reaction really freaked us all out. It was a challenge the rest of the time to keep Ella from moving around, but we were able to keep her occupied with suckers and bubbles floating around the room. She stayed the night for observation, and her blood pressure numbers were already looking better.

It looked like she had a new sense of energy. The body is so masterfully made, and it is crazy to think that if one little area is out of whack, or just a bit too small, that it can have just a huge effect on the rest of your body. She was her spunky self once again.

*"And we know that for those who love God all things work together for good."*—**Romans 8:28 (ESV)**

# Chapter 25

# BALLOON #2

Over the course of the next year, we had some sense of normalcy and structure. Still lots of doctor visits, blood pressure checks, and random vomiting. At least it seemed like the vomiting spells were getting better and a longer length of time between them. Ella's iron levels were in check, and we were able to switch her over to a pill. Hallelujah!

Noah started half-day kindergarten and was doing pretty well. Ella started preschool and enjoyed her teacher and the new friends she was making. We were connecting with people and continued to share Ella's story to help fundraise for our beloved Riley Hospital.

As the year went on, we celebrated Noah graduating from the Big K, but we were also noticing Ella's blood pressure was creeping up again. Further tests revealed the same results as the previous year. As Ella grew, her narrowing returned. So, in the summer of 2010, another balloon procedure was performed. Thankfully, we had the same calm, God-loving surgeon.

I think the nurses recalled what had happened the last time and prepared a little differently this time. Once Ella was in the recovery room, we found her legs were tapped down to the bed so she could not move them at all. I was thankful that they took this extra precaution based on the scary incident that happened the previous year. Thankfully, all went smoothly this time.

The most difficult part occurred the next day with Ella not wanting the nurse to pull off the large bandage from the incision area so we could go home. She didn't want anything to do with it. The nurse was so sweet as she approached Ella and spoke so kindly to her as Joe and I tried to convince her that it would feel better once it was off. No one likes sticky tape ripped off of them. Grandma tried to distract her with a Barbie doll she had brought for her and a juicy popsicle. The nurse would tug a little, and Ella would give her a scowl and try to move the nurses arm away. Grandma would put the popsicle in front of Ella's face, she would take a lick, the nurse would tug a little more, Ella would push her away, and here came the popsicle. This cycle went on and on until everything was off, and the nurse could happily leave the room. You could tell she had dealt with that a time or two.

Ella was definitely more aware of her surroundings now that she was almost five years old and knew what she didn't like. Once everything was off and detached, we were able to head home.

It was another successful surgery, and her blood pressure went back into a better range for her. We had in the back of our minds, though, *How often can this be done?* She had so much growing still to do.

The battle was starting to rise again in my mind, going back to the beginning and wondering if we had made the right decision on her initial surgery. Would a full bypass have been better? Would there have been a better outcome if we had gone somewhere else? Did we do enough research? One can beat oneself up so much with endless doubting and questions. Joe had to continue to remind me that we went with our gut, and we followed what God was telling us. Several doctors agreed with her procedure, and we can't drive ourselves mad with the what ifs. It goes back to wanting the best for our children and never wanting them to have to suffer like she has and not knowing what the future holds for her. We were clinging to the scripture,

*"For I know the plans I have for you, declares the Lord, plans to prosper you and not to harm you, plans to give you hope and a future."*—Jeremiah 29:11 (NIV)

# Chapter 26

# FOR THE MOMMAS

What is the best thing to do when doubt starts to creep into your head? Hit the floor! Plant those knees on the floor, by your bed, in your living room, closet, the altar at church, and pray! Ask the Lord for help with your thoughts, feelings, and insecurities. Ask for clarity to see the path ahead of you. Will it always look the way we think it should? No, but God has it under control. It took me way too long to see and realize this. Thankfully, I had a lot of help from Joe, family, and friends. Even then, it wasn't easy.

When we were in the hospital, all I had to focus on was Ella. At home, all these other factors come into play, and I felt that people were looking at me thinking, "Come on, get your crap together and get back to the way things used to be." But, it really could never be like that again. Things were different. *I'm different.* Caring for a child with unique needs will never go away. There I was though, trying to put up this front like I could do it all and had it all together. I know that I tried not to push people away purposely, but I became more insecure and the thoughts of, *I need to do this all on my own or people will think I am a failure* kept coming up. These are the lies of the devil seeping in as we try to grow closer to the Lord. That dirty guy is trying to tear us down with his lies. I know that I damaged relationships along the way. And I truly feel sorry for that.

I finally broke and let Joe in on the darkness that was encompassing me. He didn't realize how low it had gotten for me. No one did. Being around others would lift up my spirits, and it was the alone times when things would come crashing in. It was challenging to share those feelings of despair, doubt, and insecurity. I started to share with Joe and then later a few close friends. It was those first few words that just needed to spew out. "I'm hurting. I'm struggling. I'm angry that we have to deal with this. I'm upset that Ella has to suffer. I don't understand why this is all happening, and I wish I knew when it will all be okay." I welcomed the comfort and encouraging words. I remember that first evening when I opened up to Joe. He held me in a tight embrace, telling me that we were going to get through this, and he made me promise not to hold back my feelings. He was there to help me through this.

The weight did start to lift from my shoulders. I was able to function a little better as a wife, mother, and friend. Don't get me wrong, it didn't happen overnight, but at least those dark thoughts in my mind that maybe I just couldn't take it any longer, because this all just didn't seem fair, started to fade, and the light was flickering in my eyes again. On the outside, I seemed to be doing okay and doing all the right stuff. We were very involved in church, and I didn't want to be a fraud any longer. I had been a fraud in the sense that I wasn't trusting the Lord like He wanted me to. I had given in to negativity and doubt. And that had to change—for me, for our kids, for our marriage.

I also shared with my doctor my struggles. He suggested a medicine to help with the anxiety and depression. I never was one who wanted to take medicine to try to help improve my mood, but once you hit a certain low, something has to change. It helped! I was able to regain some focus on reality. I didn't want it to be a long-term thing of taking the medicine, but I do feel it was needed to help me through that phase of my life. I know there are lots of opinions on medication, from those prescribed by doctors to those considered more holistic or natural, but in my situation at the time, the medication did help me with my struggles. Everyone can have different things that help them through their struggles. The important thing is to recognize what your needs are and do what works for you. I definitely struggled with sharing this part of my journey, but I hope by sharing openly, I can help others find the strength to deal with similar issues.

I recall a time when the women at our church had a women's retreat, and I shared my story about Ella. I was pretty real about the struggles. Not sure why we as women struggle with opening up and letting others know, "Hey, I'm having a hard time and need help climbing out of this pit. Will you pray for me?" Maybe it's because we are "supposed" to seem like we have it all together? We are all human creatures who sin and need the Lord and each other to make it through the good and bad times. God made us to be relational beings, to rely on Him, and to have each other for support and to speak His truth to each other. I had felt bad because I hadn't really shared those fears with my own mom and sister. I didn't want to worry them or add stress to the already stressful circumstances. They were there when I shared at the retreat and hadn't realized the internal struggles that had happened. It ended up being a very freeing experience. I had gone through many dark days just going through the motions as my thoughts and mind went deeper and deeper into darkness and despair, which Satan loves. He loves that negativity and hopeless feeling. If you have that right now, put down the book, pick up your phone, and call your spouse, a sibling, a family member, a friend, your pastor, and share those feelings. Let them help you

*Don't let Satan win this battle, because God wants you to win the war.*

with it! Don't let Satan win this battle, because God wants you to win the war. Trust me, once you let those first few words out of your mouth to someone, healing can begin. When someone else knows your struggles, then part of that burden is lifted. It doesn't mean that you are giving your burdens to another person, because, who wants to do that? But it does mean that the person can help take that burden and release it to God. He wants you to lean on Him.

"Then you will call upon me and come and pray to me, and I will hear you."

Jeremiah 29:12 (ESV)

# Chapter 27

# GOD-CENTERED MARRIAGE

Our struggles weren't just dealing with the medical problems themselves and my inner insecurities, but it also had affected our marriage and relationship with one another. When I started sharing my heartache with Joe, that was when we were able to meet each other at the place of our loneliness. Some things were harder on Joe to deal with regarding Ella's situation. I felt like I was failing as a mother, a wife, a friend. He felt like he was failing as a husband, father, protector, and provider. And I think Joe was dealing with some jealousy as well, with more of my focus on the children than on him. I can imagine that is a struggle in a lot of relationships with children, and there is a time where the children do require more attention than the spouse. A lot of it comes with raising a family. It is certainly doable but challenging when the children are small. Throw in some medical conditions and, holy cow, it is difficult. Once we really started communicating our feelings and dealing with our own selfishness, we were able to break down the walls that had slowly been built up over the last few years and really hear each other's struggles and look for a way to mend the hurts that we were causing. I remember a few times vividly at the kitchen counter exchanging nasty words and a feeling of emptiness and disconnect. I think we were each trying to keep our heads above water, but separately, not together, and that was driving a wedge between us when we needed to hold onto each other desperately to survive the situation and be strong for each other and our family.

What we realized, though, was that we had to stay in communication. We had to lean on each other with our struggles and pray for not just what we were going through with Ella but for our marriage. This was a huge turning point in our marriage. Once the lines of language truly opened up and we knew what each of us was struggling with, then we could really deal with it and lift one another up and have that support that God wanted in our marriage. We opened up to our family group, and they were able to listen and provide support. I can't express enough how much the bond with fellow believers in Christ can help when you are going through a valley, even though it is tough being vulnerable and sharing true ugliness. God has made us to connect with one another. Thank you, Lord, for Your constant being and showing what a wonderful blessing matrimony is to be when You are at the center of it all.

*We had to lean on each other with our struggles and pray for not just what we were going through with Ella but for our marriage.*

Joe and I hold onto the lyrics from some of our favorite inspirational songs, including "Broken Together" by Casting Crowns, which is about marriage and how we are each broken in our own ways. Maybe we weren't meant to be complete, but rather broken together as long as God is in the center.

*"Trust in the Lord with all your heart and lean not on your own understanding; in all your ways submit to him, and he will make your paths straight.""*—**Proverbs 3:5-6 (NIV)**

# Chapter 28

# SIBLINGS HAVE IT ROUGH, TOO

Another dynamic that was challenging was having another child to raise. Oh, the guilt that can set in when there are a lot of times that you have to focus on the child with unique needs. Despite Ella's medical conditions, she was a pretty laidback little girl. Noah, on the other hand, was my very energetic, strong-willed child. Or as our neighbor, Dick, would say, "He is all boy." No truer of a statement.

When Noah was smaller, I tried to do playdates with mom friends and a mom's group. Unbeknownst to them, I left in tears several times, because Noah was a handful and, again, I was battling my own demons. I was realizing that Noah had some social issues and going to social events would ramp up his behavior. So, we had to do everything in stride—fewer playdates and smaller group gatherings. As time went on, it was getting harder to decipher if Noah's challenges were his own or a result of the circumstances of Ella's medical issues. Was he feeling overshadowed, unloved, or mistreated? I couldn't blame him at all. We all struggled with the prolonged and intense situation, so I could never expect a little boy to understand what all was going on when I had a hard time understanding it myself. We realized that understanding Noah was really a balancing act and truly learning how our child was designed. He had been shuffled around a lot when there were doctor visits and surgeries, although we tried to make them fun playdates with people who knew him well. Aunt Marilyn was always a good helper in watching him at her in-home daycare when needed. Somehow, she always had a knack of getting him to eat things at her house that he would never eat at home.

In the fall of 2011, the kids started at a new school, and Ella was loving kindergarten. We loved the new school, her kindergarten teacher (Mrs. Reed), and Noah's second grade teacher (Mrs. Garrett). But this was also proving to be a very difficult time for Noah. He is a very bright boy, and he was offered a spot in the high ability class. We thought this would be a good fit for him and gladly accepted. The transition wasn't easy for him, and this added to the stress of daily life. It was like he had forgotten how to read. His reading testing levels had decreased dramatically. We were working with him, meeting with his teacher, getting intervention involved. Should he stay in the class, or switch to another class? I had become obsessed with checking his grades. I think every time I sat at the computer I checked to see if anything had changed. I'm talking multiple times a day. I'm a bit embarrassed to admit that. I didn't want him to struggle and feared it would only get worse. Luckily, he had the best teacher.

I loved how organized she was and how much she poured into her students, and still does. She hadn't had to deal with this kind of situation before, but she wasn't willing to give up on him. I tried to help her out in class when I could. I wanted to be there for him the same way I was for Ella. With a lot of work, we were able to get him back on track. I'm still not sure how much of it was him or just part of the situation going on at home. And I'm sure the teachers thought I was a bit cuckoo during that year, which could have been the case also. I really felt like Noah grew up a lot during this time. One thing that we had to keep reminding ourselves was that having a child with unique needs and lifelong medical issues affects everyone in the family. We all struggled with the situation, and children see and interpret things differently than adults do. We tried to keep the lines of communication open, although some days were easier than others for that. We tried our best to keep life as "normal" as possible for him. He is a very caring boy, and thankfully we were able to make progress. We definitely learned that extra patience and grace were a necessity.

Even nowadays, a little bit of jealousy will rear its ugly head, and the kids will ask who is my favorite. I always tell them I love them the same amount, to the moon and back. They may be different and each bring joy in different ways, but I love them the same amount. Every once in a while, Noah will throw out there, "You love Ella more because she is 'special.'" Oh Noah, someday when you are a parent, you will have a better understanding.

"Grow in the grace and knowledge of our Lord and Savior Jesus Christ."

2 Peter 3:18 (NIV)

# THE START OF OUR TRANSPLANT JOURNEY

Let's bring everyone up to speed on what happened between spring and fall of 2011, shall we?

**Sunday April 17, 2011**
**Journal entry by Joe**

*Hello, everyone. We hope that this update finds everyone out there in Ella Fan Land doing well. If you couldn't tell…this is Joe. Angela and I have both been talking about updating Ella's CaringBridge, but neither of us can give an answer why we have not. I believe it's because, from the outside, Ella appears to have nothing wrong with her. We have*

*sort of been on the "highway" on cruise control. Don't get this wrong as we are fully aware of her condition. However, she has been treated for a while with success and we get used to that, I reckon. Anyway, I woke up this morning, and the kids stayed the night out at their (and our) wonderful friends' house, the Milsaps, and Angela is still getting her beauty sleep (even though she doesn't need it). I felt led to finally update everyone on our little, but quickly getting bigger, Ella.*

*First, a little update on what she's doing now.*

*Ella is five now and will be six years old in July. She is in her second year of pre-school and will be starting kindergarten in the fall. She is also in a gymnastics class and just got promoted to the next class. Angela takes her every Thursday afternoon for an hour. Her bridge is getting better every time she shows it off, and her strength is increasing. Ella's iron levels are great, and we have been able to wean her off of her iron supplement and gastro medicine. She rarely has a vomiting spell. So glad to be past all of the vomit.*

*While I'm at it, a quick update on Noah. He's seven and turns eight in September. He's really enjoying first grade this year and doing great. We have plans to play a lot more golf this summer. He and I have already been out once, and we even walked nine holes. He decided not to play baseball...even though he started to change his mind after the cut-off. He and Ella will be attending a brand-new elementary school in the fall, which is pretty cool.*

*Two weeks ago, Ella had her annual MRA/I scan. You should have seen her. Angela and I were both there for her. To witness how far she has come when accepting treatment is amazing. She willingly laid down on the table for the anesthesiologist. As he put the mask on her to administer the sleepy gas, she smiled at us as long as she could. We are so proud of her.*

*Last week, we had a follow-up appointment with Dr. Andreoli to review the results of the scan. This is where the "cruise control" comes off and it's time to make some maneuvers.*

*Remember that she only has one working kidney. The artery to that working kidney is found to be narrowed again. The last two years after the scans showed the artery was narrowed, Dr. Marshalack performed the balloon procedure to open it up. Here we*

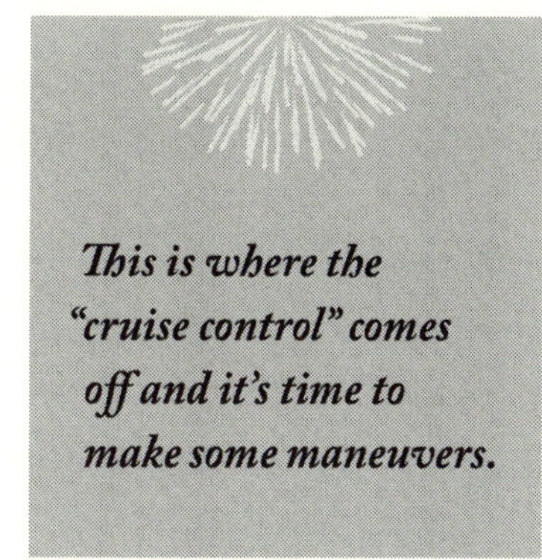


*are a third time. It›s not a surprise as the doctors shared with us that perhaps this may need to be done several times while she continues to grow. However, the scan showed the working kidney is starting to be affected by the slight decrease in blood supply as it is not getting bigger and is a little smaller since the last scan.*

*Here is the game plan...let me change that...here is what's going on in the "huddle." Four of Ella's doctors, who, in my opinion, are among the brightest on the planet when it comes to knowing kids, are going to meet and discuss options. Ultimately, keeping Ella away from major surgery until absolutely necessary is the major goal. She still has a lot of growing to do. Hopefully, that gathering of doctors will happen in the next couple of weeks. For now, Dr. Andreoli has prescribed another medication that will help her kidney to process the blood or something like that. I think Angela said it's a calcium blocker.*

*As I just finished up the last couple lines of this update, "Lifesong" by Casting Crowns came on. It reminds us that Ella's journey is God's will. For those of you who have never met, she has such a servant's heart. As our Jesus came to earth not to be served but to serve, our little Ella is all HIS. Oh, mighty*

*GOD, we are reminded yet again how precious a gift has been given to us, the gift of children. How You must have felt for Your Son, Jesus. For those of you who might have doubt in believing in the Creator of the universe and the ULTIMATE gift given to us, HIS SON JESUS, and for those of you who desire FREEDOM from fear, loneliness, guilt, and all the other things that come from being in this world— there is HOPE. There is an ANSWER. There is LOVE waiting for you. For others reading this post who have accepted the ULTIMATE gift Jesus Christ, join me in turning off the "cruise control"...as most of us have some kind of cruise control.... and start driving on PURPOSE...HIS PURPOSE.*

*We will post something when we hear back from the doctors. Thanks to all who have continued to ask about Ella and keep Ella and us in your prayers. God bless you all, and we love you.*

*Joe*

Tuesday, June 14, 2011
Journal entry by Angela

*So emotional! I have been so emotional lately. Little things, big things, everything! I really need to get a grip! Parenting is so hard! It is the toughest job I will ever have! You know you always want the best for*

*your kids and you want to instill in them good values, how to make good decisions, how to be all around good kids, but kids will be kids! Throw in some medical issues and all-around chaos, and you have a lot of grey hairs growing on my head!*

*Some big decisions in the making for Miss Ella. The doctors have reviewed Ella's chart and are considering an "auto" kidney transplant. They have referred her info to the kidney transplant doctor at Riley. He wanted another test for further viewing (a 3D CAT scan), which she had done last week. She actually did pretty well, only a few tears.*

*Tomorrow we have an appointment at Riley with Dr. Brown (surgeon who did her first surgery), Dr. Darragh (cardiology), and hopefully Dr. Goggins (kidney transplant doctor) and Dr. Andreoli (kidney). I will find out for sure in the morning who all can make it. We have a lot of questions we need answered and to find out the CAT scan results and the proposal for action.*

*I have spoken with the transplant coordinator and an auto kidney transplant is actually two surgeries in one. They would take out Ella's right functioning kidney, re-construct the renal artery (which has the narrowing) then transplant it to her pelvic area, attaching it to the aorta where there can be proper blood flow to the kidney.*

*The reasoning behind this option is because Ella's kidney has not grown over the past year and has even gotten smaller. They need to do what makes sense to preserve her functioning kidney and give it the best chance possible to thrive. From what I gather from Dr. Andreoli, the benefit would be better blood flow for her kidney to function better, eliminate yearly balloon procedures, and get rid of the narrowed part of the renal artery. We should learn more tomorrow.*

*It was a little hard to imagine at first. We were antici-pating maybe another balloon procedure, not major surgery. I am feeling bad at the thought of putting her through another surgery. She is acting very well and is such a vibrant five-year-old. It is hard to imagine all this "stuff" is going on inside her.*

*I talked with Dr. Ho the other day, and he was reassuring that the Riley doctors know Ella as they have cared for her for the past five years. He also feels they need to do what they need to do to preserve her right kidney.*

*Thank you all for your continued support and prayers! ~Angela*

It was a small miracle that we were able to get all of the doctors together for a meeting to discuss the potential next steps for Ella. They were all very busy people, and we felt very grateful that they were able to make time for this to happen. As we listened to their great minds talk about Ella and what is in her best interest, we were certainly in the presence of some pretty smart people. It was Dr. Darragh's incredible idea for the auto (meaning

*He wanted a back-up plan in case it didn't work out.*

"self") kidney transplant, and Dr. Goggins really believed it could be done. What they were proposing was transplanting her kidney to another location in her abdomen and surgically attaching her kidney to another blood vessel attached to her aorta that would offer a stronger blood supply to make sure her remaining kidney had the best chance of maintaining blood flow to keep it growing and functioning. He expressed that he had never done this surgery before, but with Ella's history and current status, he thought it could be a success. He looked at me and stated that if he was going to attempt this, he wanted a back-up plan in case it didn't work out. He wanted me to be tested to see if I was a match for Ella in case she needed a regular kidney transplant. Typically, the mother has a higher chance of being a match than the father, so that is where they wanted to start.

My eyes widened as a feeling of, *This surgery is for real going to happen* came over me. I expressed nervousness but explained I would do anything he needed for our little girl. Joe, thinking of the possibility of his daughter and his wife both having major surgery, asked Dr. Goggins, "If you were to give a percentage of a success rate, what would it be?" He replied, "90-95%." We would both admit that Dr. Goggins had an arrogant confidence about him, but it is the kind of confidence that you want in a surgeon. It was a deal. Everyone was on board, and we started scheduling appointments for testing. The first step was to find out if I was a match for her.

The next few weeks were daunting as we waited anxiously for the results of the blood work and scan testing. *Oh Lord, what do you have in store for us? If it is your will, please let me be a match for Ella. I will gladly give her a kidney to help make her life lived better.* Then, we received a call from Mary Lynn, the transplant coordinator. The initial testing showed I was a match! I just broke down in tears with gratefulness. One way or another, Ella would be getting a good functioning kidney. Mary Lynn shared there were still several tests that Ella and I would have to go through, but initially all looked good. Now, it was a matter of finding out whether my left or right kidney would be better for her as to the healthiness of the kidneys and size. I was completely fine with that. Bring on the tests. Let's get this going!

Although we felt confident with the doctor's ability, still the unknown was scary. What if it didn't go perfectly like the first surgery? The what if's can circle and circle like a tornado building momentum looking for its next tree to demolish. We felt it best to seek a second opinion again, so we headed over to the Children's Hospital in Ohio to see another well-known surgeon. She reviewed all of Ella's medical records and agreed with Dr. Goggins. She reassured us that we were in great hands at Riley and would not suggest moving her anywhere else. It was great comfort to hear that. As Joe explained it, when dealing with something this major, you want the Babe Ruth of surgeons working on your daughter. You want that confidence, the person who is going to point to the outfield, letting everyone know that he is going to knock this out of the park. So, forward with the testing.

We had been through so much over those past five years that I had to keep the thought of my own possible surgery and recovery shoved away in the back of my mind. During one particular test, I just couldn't hold it together any more. Ella had been through this test just a few days earlier. It was a kidney scan where she had to lay very still. The machine circled the lower half of her body, and they moved the platform she was laying on to just the right spot for imaging. They needed some before and after pictures with dye contrast. I was sitting right by Ella's side. I started to sing, "You Are My Sunshine" to keep her mind off of what was going on. She would look at me with those big, grey-blue eyes and a little grin on her face. I just loved those little dimples on either side of her smile. The first set of pictures were done and they needed to push in the dye through her IV. The nurse told her it would feel warm and make her feel like she had to pee, but not to worry. She wouldn't go potty. It was just her bladder filling up. Once the dye was going in, the look changed on Ella's face and worry took over. She looked up at me saying, "I have to go potty." I told her, "It's okay, you're not going to go potty. It just feels funny. Just relax, baby doll." They quickly adjusted the platform again for more pictures, and I started making up a story to try to distract her again. She stated again, "I have to go potty now." I assured her we would go in a few minutes. Thankfully, the test was done within a few minutes, and we quickly got her dressed and to the bathroom. She was very relieved that the test was over. It was certainly harder to keep her calm and still during these tests while she was awake and now six years old.

A few days later, it was my turn for the same test. Ella was not with me to comfort me, though. It was the same small, dimly-lit room. I laid on the same platform and moved into the circular machine for the initial pictures. All I could think about was Ella laying in that same spot and realizing what she had felt. Then they put the dye in, and there really was a warm feeling that came with it as my kidney was filling up my bladder, and I did really feel like I was going to pee my pants. I couldn't hold back the emotions and tears just started falling down my checks and then hitting my ears as I was still lying down. I tried to contain it but couldn't. Every test that Ella had been through, I could only helplessly sit by her and try to reassure her that all was okay and would be okay, without really knowing what she was feeling or going through. But now I felt what she had felt, and it was scary and uncontrollable. The sweet nurse came over to check on me and see if she could help as, obviously, I was not okay. She was very empathetic to the situation. She stayed with me with her hand on my shoulder, tears in her own eyes, wiping away my own until I was able to regain my composure. When I was able to get up, she hugged me tightly and reassured me, "It's going to be okay."

All was looking pretty good. I was confirmed a match! This made us feel even more confident going into the surgery process. From the testing, they decided the right kidney would be the better one to transplant. One of the last doctors I needed to visit was a Riley psychologist. She was very pleasant. This was a routine appointment for all potential kidney donors. I understood all the risks involved and was very willing to go through with it. I wish I would have been able to open up more to her, but I just wasn't feeling it as she was a stranger, and, thankfully, I had such a strong family to lean on.

*Crying out for just another miracle with our sweet girl.*

Joe and I had also met with Pastor Randy and Lisa on multiple occasions. They listened to our hearts, heard our fears, and encouraged us. Prayed with us fervently. Many occasions we sat at the altar on a Sunday morning, worshiping God for His blessings and crying out for just another miracle with our sweet girl and to keep our family strong through yet another valley. I lifted up Noah as well. Though I may never fully understand why, faith was what kept us going, and God's promises. We couldn't be more thankful for our loving family, always willing to drop things at a moment's notice to help out, and our friends who had become like family over the last few years.

*God's timing is never late. Never early. He's always right on time, and His plans for you are good.*

# Chapter 30

# DR. GOGGINS' OFFICE

It was a week before surgery, and it was time to visit with Dr. Goggins and Mary Lynn to go over the surgery information and get answers to any questions we had. It seemed a bit weird to be in his actual office instead of a patient room. There was a desk, a couple of chairs, and a little couch. Several accomplishment plaques on the wall and paperwork covered his desk. Both Dr. Goggins and Mary Lynn were very comforting about the upcoming procedure. The incision would be the same as Ella's first surgery (down her belly), except longer now that she was bigger and they had to work in a larger area. He explained that they would remove her left kidney, since it was no longer functioning, take out her right kidney and get rid of the narrowed area, then reconstruct the artery to make it nice and big and transplant it to her lower pelvic area so it will have a good source of blood flow. If all went well, my kidney wouldn't be needed, but I would be on standby in case it didn't take. For some reason, an ease and peace came over me. I really felt that it was going to work and my kidney would not be needed.

Dr. Goggins did explain that her kidney had been under so much pressure her whole life, that even if this worked, she might still need a regular kidney transplant in the future. But who knows what will be available in the future as far as the medical field goes. We were just focusing on the here and now and what was best for sweet girl.

We had a good sense about Dr. Goggins' ability. We appreciated his down-to-earth, tell-it-like-it-is, kind personality. Toward the end of our meeting that day, I asked him if he played music in the operating room, or what he did to focus. His response: "I listen to music. I like all kinds—Jimmy Hendrix, Eminem." My initial response was to giggle a bit before I proceeded to tell him, "Ella likes Christian music." He replied with a grin that he liked some Jeremy Camp and Michael W. Smith. Joe told him that Ella's favorite song was "Lifesong" by Casting Crowns—a song very near and dear to our hearts.

I think he took that in stride. I guess the momma in me couldn't imagine my little girl unconsciously listening to some heavy metal band or rapper while a life-saving procedure was being performed on her. I'm not trying to knock different music genres, as I like all kinds, but that wasn't the time for it, in my mind. We ended our time with hugs, and off we walked down the beige, echoey hallway, feeling good but nervous at the same time. The thought of another not well-known procedure being performed on

Ella was bubbling in our heads. We kept reminding ourselves that God's got this!

The blood work had been drawn. I think Ella and I both felt a bit weak in the knees after giving that many vials of blood. I swear there were at least

twenty for each of us. All the prep work was completed. The countdown was on.

Now it was time to sit Noah and Ella down and really explain what was about to happen. Ella was used to lots of tests and giving blood, but now that she was older, she would be able to understand that she would be having surgery and have to stay in the hospital for several days. Joe did a great job explaining to her why she needed the surgery and how it was going to help her. We weren't exactly sure what was going through her mind, but the tears started to well up in her eyes, and she told us she didn't want to have any shots or stay in the hospital. As we all cried and hugged each other, we comforted her and told her we would be right there by her side and she was going to do great with this surgery. We prayed that she would have peace and that God would be watching over her. She went to bed that night very teary-eyed as I am sure her own anxiety was building a bit.

The Sunday before surgery, we shared at church about Ella's upcoming procedure. Many of our church family gathered around us, laying hands on Ella and praying for protection and healing. With Ella right between us, she looked around with those big blue eyes in awe at everyone, soaking in all the love. Noah held on tight to our side as we were huddled all together. One of the elders anointed Ella's forehead with oil, and we ended the service lifting up our prayers. The power of prayer is an amazing thing.

We couldn't have asked for a better send-off before we made our way down to Indianapolis.

*"Let my lifesong sing to you."*
—Lyrics from "Lifesong" by Casting Crowns

# Chapter 31

# THE TRANSPLANT IS UNDERWAY

Just after midnight on October 10, 2011, not a lot of sleep was happening. Another major surgery. What if it didn't work? Another recovery. Would it be harder on her? I was finally able to drift off to sleep when the alarm sounded and startled me awake at 5:00 a.m. It was time. Time for Joe and me to gather our bags and head off to the hospital. We had stayed the night at Stacie and Jim's house since they lived in Indy and we wouldn't have to get up quite as early. We scooped Ella up as she was sleeping so soundly and buckled her into her car seat. We left their house at about 5:20 and arrived to check-in at about 5:55. The nerves were starting to build.

All checked in and waiting in the small prep room with the curtain pulled, Joe was reading a book to Ella who was curled up on his lap in that cute pediatric gown and non-slip socks on her feet. I signed the last of the paperwork. I felt as if I was signing my life away. Roy, Connie, and Stacie arrived at about 6:45 a.m. and sat with us as we were visited by different nurses, the anesthesiologist, and the Child Life Specialist. We had seen her before, and she enjoyed seeing Ella again, although we all wished it had been under different circumstances. Ella was able to decorate her mask that would help her go to sleep when she arrived in the operating room. It had googly eyes on it, and Ella chose root beer flavored Chapstick again for the "lips."

The nurse came over to let us know it was almost time. We all gathered around Ella to pray for her just as Dr. Goggins walked over to see how we were doing. Ella said, "Hi, Dr. Goggins." She must have really liked him if she talked to him. She really didn't talk to too many of her doctors. I asked Dr. Goggins if he was well-rested and feeling good. We didn't want a sleepy or ill doctor on our hands. With a grin, he assured us that he was ready.

We asked him if he would like to join us in prayer, and he was happy to do so. Ella being center stage, we circled around her, joining hands. Dr. Goggins put his hand on her little head. Joe prayed a special prayer over Ella, Dr. Goggins, and all the nurses who would be taking care of her. It brought us all to tears, but in our hearts, we could feel that God was going to guide the doctors' hands through this all. When the prayer was over, Dr. Goggins got his phone out and brought something up on the screen. The nurse was with us at this point, and he showed his phone to her and asked her to have this playing when Ella went into the operating room. Then he showed us. It was Casting Crowns' "Lifesong." Oh, my goodness, I just wanted to melt on the floor in a puddle. He had remembered our conversation and Ella's song. I knew right then that Ella had a very special place in his heart.

Ella received hugs and kisses all around, and she went a bit reluctantly to the nurse. Joe and I embraced as we watched her being taken through those double doors clutching her pink and white blanket at about 7:40 that morning. We grabbed a sandwich from the café and made our way up to the second floor to get settled in for the day. We checked in with the nurse just like we had five years prior. We knew it would be about an hour before the first nurse update. We were so blessed that day to have several friends and family there to support us—Mom, Skip, Roy, Connie, Shari, Stacie, Jim, Chris, Jessica, Scott, Kirsten, Jeremy, Tina, and Pastor Randy. Our hearts felt so full with all the love and support. This time around was also different with the aspect of social media. In 2006, we mainly had to call people to update them or post something on the CaringBridge site. Now there was texting and Facebook—more avenues to keep everyone updated quickly. We passed the time with good conversation and some snacks that Jessica had brought for everyone. We were so thankful for family and friends to pick up the pieces and fill in the spots that we just didn't have in us to think about. And again, I knew Noah was in good hands and being well taken care of.

Another aspect of the day that had been swirling in the back of Roy, Connie, and Shari's minds was that Sheryl was also six years old when her last major surgery was performed. They couldn't help but feel that pressure build up, and they didn't want Ella to have the same outcome. Although this surgery was different from Ella's first surgery and from Sheryl's surgery, it still was major surgery, and we couldn't bear the thought of the Lord taking her from us. We all anxiously awaited the nurse's first update.

The surgical nurse rounded the corner at 9:20 a.m. Ella had been in the operating room at about 8:40 a.m., and they were just getting started. Ella did great going to sleep, and they had an IV in her left foot and left hand and a central line on the left side of her neck. We were relieved to know that things were underway and starting off well.

About an hour later came the second update. The left kidney had been removed, and they were starting to go to the right side. Ella's pressures looked good. No concerns. After each visit with good news, we were able to exhale a bit more.

At 11:25 a.m. came the third update. Dr. Goggins was working on the right renal artery. It was out on the table, and they were starting the reconstruction process. It was strange to imagine our daughter's organ just hanging out on a table and the doctor manipulating it. The nurse reassured all was going well. As soon as she walked away, I updated my journal and sent out a quick update to Ella's groupies.

The next update was at 12:30 p.m. Ella was still doing well. The reconstruction was complete, and they were sewing the right kidney back in. The nurse was not sure exactly where the new placement was going to be. I gave such a sigh of relief knowing the end was getting closer. We ate some of the food that Jessica had so graciously brought for everyone and patiently waited for the next update.

The nurse's fifth and final update was at 1:50 p.m., and the doctor was closing up. Everything went well, and Dr. Goggins would be up in a bit to chat with us.

I felt the need to journal again. I didn't want to miss anything that might be important information later. With each good report from the nurse, a little more stress lifted from my body. Having such sweet friends and family there this time really made the time go by quickly. I still couldn't get over the fact that these people sacrificed and took time off from work and out of their lives to be the hands and feet of Jesus and to comfort us as they did. I will never forget and always strive to pass that on to bless others.

Ella was out of surgery, and the nurse told us that Dr. Goggins would be up shortly to discuss with us how the surgery went. About twenty minutes later, we saw Dr. Goggins approaching. A huge knot formed in my stomach. What was he going to say? Would it be the good news we were hoping for? The knot grew bigger and bigger. Joe and I stood up to greet him, and we were very eager for his words. The rest of our group was listening intently as he began to speak.

I was a little surprised by his demeanor. He seemed nervous as he was shifting his weight from one foot to the other. He ran his hands through his hair and started by saying, "All looks pretty good, but that was the most difficult surgery I have ever

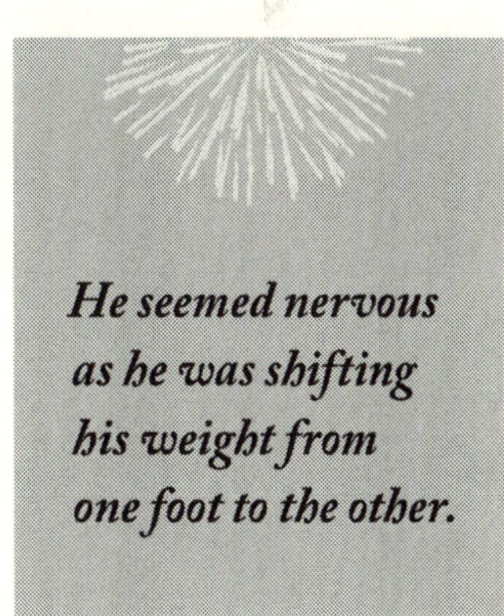

*He seemed nervous as he was shifting his weight from one foot to the other.*

done. The vessels were so small. I used the smallest suture that I have ever used. I don't want to do that surgery again." Okay. Not quite the canter I was expecting, but yet again, I welcomed his honesty. He proceeded to tell us the main artery branched off into smaller arteries. So, this made it more challenging with the reconstruction process. He transplanted her right kidney into a lower right area of her body to guarantee better blood flow. The left kidney was easy to remove. He was also telling us that Ella's bladder was huge. He referred to it as a "trucker's bladder," as they hold it for longer periods of time. He advised us to have her pee more often. He did reassure us that he thought everything looked good. He would do an ultrasound to check the blood flow, and, as long as she peed, it would be a good sign. We would know more in the next few hours and days.

Our initial relief was over. She made it through the surgery. Now we were just praying it was a success. I am pretty sure I had never prayed so hard for my daughter to pee. We did really appreciate Dr. Goggins' honesty about the situation and him not downplaying anything. We wanted the truth. The knot was still there, but it had decreased in size.

*His demeanor had done a 180.*

About thirty minutes later, Dr. Goggins returned, and his demeanor had done a 180. You could see the huge relief on his face, a smile, and he was settled in his stance. He reported, "The ultrasound looks great, and she is peeing buckets!" Praise the Lord! That was the news that we had been hoping for! We gave Dr. Goggins big hugs. I'm sure the rest of the floor could tell by our cheers that we had received good news. He seemed very hopeful that all was going to be well. The next few days would be very crucial. We should be able to see Ella in less than an hour. Dr. Goggins did explain to us that this was a first for Riley to have a child who had an autologous kidney transplant, and because it was her own kidney, not a donor, she would not have to take anti-rejection meds. So, if the nurses asked or talked about anti-rejection meds, we were to tell them that Ella under no circumstances was to have those and remind them to look at the chart. He further explained that the nurses would not have seen this type of situation before.

As he walked away, the knot became even smaller. We all hugged with cheerful hearts. Now that Ella was out of surgery and stable, a few people left to go home to be with their children and loved ones. Ella would pretty much be out the rest of the night, so no need for too many visitors. We could keep everyone updated on how she was doing. After we updated social media and sent texts to a few close friends, Joe and I sat there waiting somewhat impatiently to see Ella. We looked at each other with so much thankfulness in our hearts. This little girl was really something special and God had big plans for her. We just didn't know yet what that looked like.

The nurse arrived and escorted us down and around the hallways where we could see her in recovery at about 4:20 p.m. We had a hard time staying behind the nurse as we just wanted to rush by and get to her as quickly as we could. The recovery area was a large room lined with beds of sick children who had just had some type of procedure or operation. Your heart can't help but go out to all of those kids and their families. We locked eyes on Ella in the far bed. She was still asleep and had good color. Her heart rate and blood pressure looked great. She looked like such a sweet angel lying there so still, wrapped in her pink and while blanket. I'm sure everyone learned quickly what a comfort that blanket was to her. We just stood there staring at her, the nurse reassuring us that she did very well. She did need a blood transfusion as her hemoglobin dropped, but not a lot, and it was looking good now.

Just a short time later, she was transferred to the ninth floor of the new Riley wing. It was the new kidney transplant floor. They were able to handle intensive care now on the same floor. As we walked in, we thought, *Wow! This is a nice room.* It was only one of the few floors opened in the new wing. It was so spacious, with a pullout couch and a recliner, her own TV and mini fridge, and her own bathroom. It felt like we were back on the heart floor, but a newer version of the room. We were thankful that we could stay in this room for her whole stay instead of having to move rooms. It really brought me back to five years earlier when they were just beginning to build this wing. We could see out of Ella's room over to the area where they were just digging the hole for it at that point. Now there we were in one of the finished rooms.

Nurse Sarah greeted us at about 5:20 p.m. as we entered the room. There Ella was lying in that big bed with a small light on just behind her. We gently gave kisses on her forehead. It seemed like she had tubes everywhere, monitoring her heart, blood pressure, IV, and oxygen canal, and a tube coming out of her nose to suction out her stomach acid. Thankfully, a ventilator was not needed this time. We were hoping that she would be able to rest through the night, but about ten minutes later, her eyes started to open and eyebrows furrowed.

She whispered and nurse Sarah showed her the pain chart that had faces on it. Number one had a happy face, and as the numbers increased to ten, the faces became more sad until the ten which was clearly unhappy and in pain. Her little finger with the O2 monitor on raised up and pointed to the ten face. We could tell she was enduring a lot of pain. Sarah called the doctor, and they prescribed a higher pain medicine. It seemed to help quickly. She also had a pain medicine pump that could be pushed every fifteen minutes. Seeing her in pain just broke our hearts.

*Her little finger with the O2 monitor on raised up and pointed to the ten face.*

Thankfully, the meds helped control the pain, and she was able to rest. A few family members came in for a quick visit, kisses, and love, and then they left for the evening. It had been such a long and emotionally-draining day.

At about 7:00 p.m., it was nurse shift-change time and we met Nurse Andrea who would be taking care of Ella.

The nurses started discussing Ella's meds, and you could tell they were quickly becoming confused as to why there wasn't an order for anti-rejection meds.

I interjected and explained what type of surgery they were dealing with. Neither had heard of the possibility of an auto kidney transplant. Amazed and relieved at the same time, I think they were even more intrigued with being Ella's caregivers. They double-checked the list of prescriptions with the doctor and all was squared away.

Finally, around 9:00 p.m., we were able to settle in for the night. Ella was resting comfortably, and I drifted off to sleep on the pullout couch, thanking God for His many blessings and breathing a sigh of relief.

The next few days were filled with lots of monitoring and resting. Ella's blood pressure would go up and down, and there was lots of adjusting of meds and checking urine output. Dr. Goggins visited every day, which impressed us so much. It wasn't just the resident team making rounds. He, himself, checked on her. You could tell there was such a connection between the two of them. He would get down at Ella's level and talk to her and check to see how she was really doing. Ella definitely had her cranky times. Her eyebrows would go down, and she would crinkle her nose. When that began to happen, we would check the pain chart and

*He would get down at Ella's level and talk to her and check to see how she was really doing.*

sure enough it was time for more pain meds. Her nurses were so sweet and really on top of things. They oohed and aahed over Ella and her sweet personality. At about day three, she felt like sitting up when the Cheer Guild Treasure Castle came around and brought in a couple of figurines to paint and books to color in. There were only so many movies to watch, although we fell in love with Disney's *Tangled,* and I swear we watched it 100 times while we were there.

Ella held on to her squeeze pillow when she felt pain in her belly, but she was able to sit up enough to paint a cute cupcake money bank with a cherry on top. It ended up a colorful pink and purple. She was becoming quite the artist. Just the small amounts of movements would wear her out, though, so it was back to resting and watching Rapunzel swing around, singing songs and holding onto her long blonde hair.

On day four, Dr. Goggins felt that Ella was finally ready to be able to have something to drink and eat. Poor baby girl had just been fed liquids through the IV since the surgery. He was trying to wait as long as possible to avoid upsetting her stomach. He didn't want anything to undo the work that had been done. The evening before, she had only been able to suck some water from a sponge to wet her mouth. Unfortunately, when she drank some water, she must have had a little too much too quickly as she threw it up. I felt so bad for her. It had to have been painful to her incision area. That was what Dr. Goggins was trying to avoid so it wouldn't cause her any pain, yet that was where we ended up. Thankfully, it was just the one time, and she recovered like a champ.

The next day, Dr. Goggins felt confident that she would be able to keep something down. He told Ella she could try whatever she wanted. He asked her, "Would you like ice cream or a popsicle?" She answered, "Ice cream." And ice cream it was. She was able to enjoy it without any issues.

"Your word is a lamp
to guide my feet and
a light for my path."

Psalm 119:105 (NLT)

# Chapter 32

# GETTING HER SPUNK BACK

Day six after her surgery, she was up for a popsicle. Grape was the flavor of choice. I bet that grape popsicle was the best tasting popsicle ever! Oh, the look on her face. The blue in her eyes was getting brighter by the minute. About that time, our dear friends, the Milsaps, came in for a visit. That didn't stop Ella from enjoying that popsicle. Ella's bestie, Helene, had picked out an adorable card for her that played a catchy tune when it opened. As they were showing it to her, with the popsicle in one hand and a cute little fist with the other, she wrinkled her nose with a big, purple-lipped smile on her face and started moving her head gently back and forth

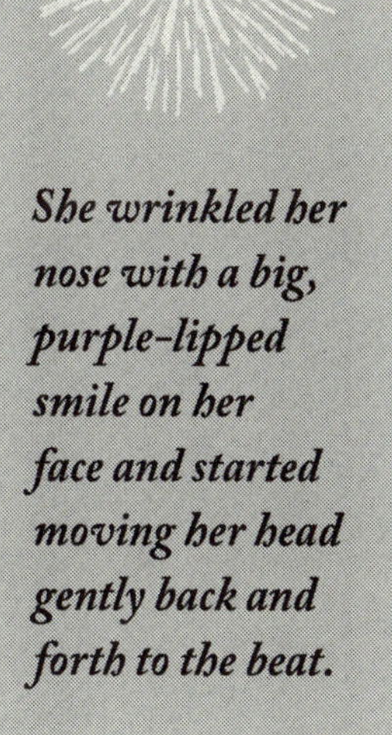

*She wrinkled her nose with a big, purple-lipped smile on her face and started moving her head gently back and forth to the beat.*

to the beat. She was getting her spunk back. We opened that card over and over, and each time, it produced the same reaction from Ella. What made her purple smile even funnier was that she had lost one of her front teeth right before having surgery. That thing had been so loose, either the breathing tube was going to knock it out or we would pull it and let the tooth fairy leave some money for it. Thankfully, the tooth fairy was able to visit just in time.

We enjoyed having so many family and friends visit those first several days. Ella enjoyed riding in the red wagon with her cousins, Samantha and Torie. We would wheel them around and drag the pole of monitors and IVs with us. Those things didn't stop us from having a good time and visiting the playroom. The gifts of stuffed animals were gaining more room on her bed. She didn't mind one bit and loved every one of them. Seeing our church family being there for us this time was such a blessing. The prayer and encouragement were like none other.

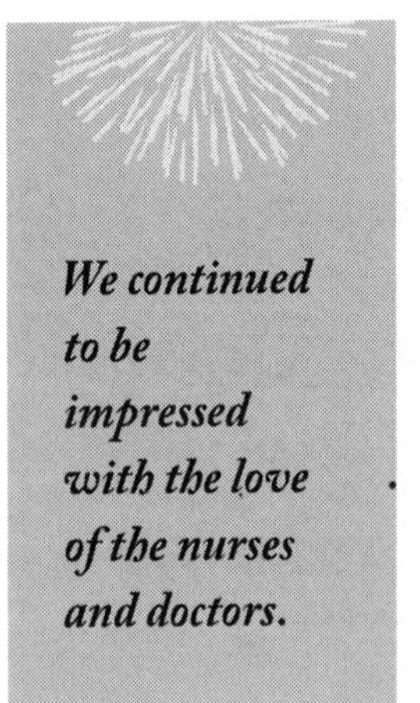


We continued to be impressed with the love of the nurses and doctors. Every nurse treated Ella like she was their own. When it was time for Ella to start walking and moving around, I couldn't have asked for better help from our nurse. We stood her on the floor and fixed her little pink hospital gown and put on her little non-slip socks. I tried my best to keep her hair under control and had braided the top part of it before surgery, but it was getting good and greasy by now and sticking out everywhere. She put her right arm across her tummy for extra support and held my hand with her left. The nurse pulled the IV stand alongside of us. Ella scooted her little feet slowly, one foot in front of the other out of her room. We made our way to the little playroom closest to her room. The nurse was encouraging her along the way, and we were praising these little accomplishments. Her eyes lit up when she saw the baby doll laying in the room. There was also a little wood-crafted MRI machine sitting in the corner. Ella was immediately drawn to it with the baby doll in one hand and her other still protecting her tummy. She laid the doll on the cushioned tray and moved it gently back and forth as if performing a test on her. Such a caring heart! I could visualize her in that moment as a young adult in scrubs with a Riley badge caring for a young girl much like herself with such compassion in her heart. I just can't help but think that someday she will be giving back to others like herself.

We enjoyed some playtime and coloring, then it was time to make our way back to the room. It had been a big exercise day. The next day, big brother was coming to visit.

Noah strolled into the room like he owned the place. We had tried our best to keep him on his normal routine. He was still going to school and things were really looking up for him. This day was all about the kiddos being together. He wanted to climb into that big bed and see what it was all about. We just reminded him to be gentle with Ella. We could tell that he sensed what she had been through. Noah is typically a rough and tumble, energetic boy, but he was being super cautious and caring with his little sister. They hung out in Ella's bed together for a bit and checked out the room. Then it was time for our daily walk, and Ella wanted to show Noah the big playroom, which was down the long hall and on the other side of the main nurses' station. We were set and ready to go. She was still taking it slow but seemed more confident in her steps. About halfway down the hall, her little sock had worked its way half off her foot, and as we stopped to help adjust it, Noah bent down to take care of it for her. I held her steady as she raised her leg, and Noah pulled her sock back up to where it was supposed to be. That small act of kindness from Noah to Ella just melted my heart. It's those little moments of love that you hold on to and cherish.

As we neared the nurses' station, we were greeted by surprised looks on the nurses' faces as they knew how far Ella had walked on her own. They gave a few cheers, and then a big smile appeared on Ella's face. We finally reached the big playroom, and Ella quickly found another baby doll to love on while Noah checked out the other toys and games in the room. After some playtime, Nurse Andrea helped us back down the hallway and into the room. What a triumphant day it was. Sweet girl was good and tired after all that. We celebrated with some micro-wave popcorn and watching none other than *Tangled*.

**October 18, 2011**
*Angela's Personal Journal*

*The doctors and nurses continue to be amazed by you. You have this inner fight in you that God has blessed you with. You really have defied all odds from where you started to where we are now. Your blood pressure continues to fluctuate, so you are still on some medicines, but we are praying that as time goes along, we can keep decreasing those blood pressure medicines until God fully heals you.*

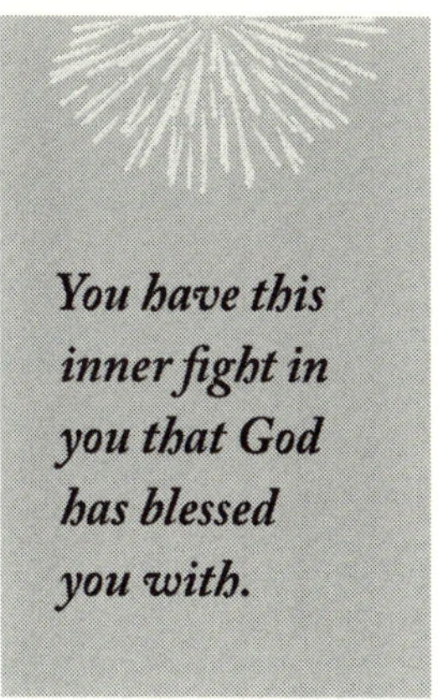


*There has been only one day that Dr. Goggins hasn't visited, and I am positive that he needed that day off. It really is something that your doctor has personally come by to see you this much. Such a testament to how devoted the Riley doctors are.*

*You were pleased to have your hair washed today. Nurse Erika and I took you on a little trip to a bathing room that had one of those cool hairdresser chairs in it, and we were able to gently wash your hair. I could tell you felt very relieved to have that done. You definitely looked more like your cute, adorable self.*

*Another sweet thing is that your night nurse, Andrea, gave you a big surprise tonight. You had told her that when Dr. Goggins says it is okay, that you really want to get your ears pierced, so she bought you your first starter earrings. When you opened the bag, your eyes widened so much and a huge smile came over your face. You were so shocked, as was I. You gave her the biggest hug. It was such a sweet and thoughtful thing for her do to. Another reason why we love our Riley nurses! They are so selfless.*

One evening, Ella was not ready to go to sleep—at all. I, on the other hand, was tired. We had been in the hospital for over a week. With so many friendly faces from visitors and daily rounds with the doctors and nurses, this momma was wearing down. Don't get me wrong, Ella and I enjoyed the company, but when nighttime hit, I was drained. Ella was off the IV and monitors and was able to take oral medicines. So this meant she was much more mobile and her bounce back from having a major surgery was remarkable. This particular night, I dimmed the lights, and we were trying to settle in with watching a movie with the volume playing softly. In an attempt to keep her in her bed, I pushed the recliner as close as I could to the bed, so I could hold her hand after I had tucked her in with her blanket. She was in a big girl bed this time and could get in and out more freely. I apparently dozed off sooner than she did, and the little booger snuck out of her bed and slid out the door to go and play with the nurse. The nurse was working on her computer right by our room, and Ella crawled underneath the small desk and made up a storyline that the nurse went along with. They were having a hay day in make-believe land.

When I awoke and realized Ella was gone, a bit of panic came over me as I peered out the door. A sheepish grin appeared on Ella's face as she asked if they could play for just a couple more minutes. How could I say no to that? The sweet thing was finally feeling well enough to play, one of her favorite things to do, so I explained that she could have a few more minutes, then it was time for bed. I think they both were happy with the response.

On day ten, Dr. Goggins came into the room and scooped Ella up and asked her if she was ready to go home. Wow! That nervous knot just shot back into my gut. *Really? Are we ready?* I knew she was feeling better, but her medicines were still being adjusted. He reassured me that she was ready and so was I. Her body was adjusting beautifully to her auto transplant. I would be able to handle the at-home care perfectly fine. An important sign of her recovery was monitoring her weight and blood pressure. She needed to be staying at the same weight or starting to gain, so we would weigh her twice a day and check blood pressure twice a day. At this point, we had a doppler machine that made it so much easier to check her blood pressure. I didn't have to take her to the pediatric floor to have it checked. We were able to check it in the comfort of our home. We would also have frequent visits with Dr. Goggins.

We were all excited with the news! We returned home and felt all the love from family and friends as, once again, they were blessing us with prepared meals, offers of help, and many prayers. Ella was growing, and as she healed, her blood pressure continued to drop into a normal range for a child her age. After about six weeks, Ella returned to kindergarten to finish out her year. I think I was more emotional dropping her off this time for school than I was on the first day of school. It was like a whole new beginning. A God-answered beginning.

*"As incredibly unique as her issues were, having to operate on her main big 'pipe' that supplies all the blood to her lower body and then having to go back and transplant her remaining kidney to a better blood supply within her own abdomen from the compromised kidney blood vessels, both types of faith—faith in the watchful higher power and faith in modern medicine—made me never worry that she wouldn't make it through them."*—Dr. Ho

# Chapter 33

# FEELING SAPPY

**Tuesday, May 22, 2012**
**Journal entry by Angela**

*T*ime *flies when you're having fun, and just busy! I feel like I have lots to report. First, I need to back up a bit to a couple of appointments we had in March.*

*We saw Dr. Goggins. Ella was excited to see him. Her labs were great that day, iron and hemoglobin levels were in normal ranges, kidney function levels looking good. He thought her incision was healing nicely. He said that for as complex as Ella is, this is the best outcome that we could have asked for. I would have to agree with that! A huge thank you to Dr. Goggins for his care and compassion for his patients and his knowledge and talent to be able to help children! Ella's blood pressure has NEVER been better. It has consistently been in the mid-90s. Dr. Goggins said he would just see her back in a year. He said as long as Dr. Andreoli would be seeing Ella, he was fine with her taking over treatment. It is kind of hard to think about not seeing him for a whole year. We really have made some great bonds with several doctors and nurses at Riley.*

> **He said that for as complex as Ella is, this is the best outcome that we could have asked for.**

*The next week, we saw Dr. Andreoli, and she was also very pleased with everything, and we even cut Ella's blood pressure medicine in half. Holy cow! If things continue to go well, she may even try to take her off the blood pressure medication altogether. We will see what Dr. A thinks at the June visit. A huge thank you also goes to Dr. Andreoli. She has been a huge part of Ella's health from the very beginning.*

*It still amazes me how well Ella is doing! She really, truly is a miracle girl. I am so thankful for the people God has placed in our lives to care for her, everyone who has helped us along the way, people who have prayed for her and us, amazing family and friends who have always been available at a moment's notice when we needed them, and an incredible church family.*

*It has been a very long year. It seemed like last year was so full of the unknowns and difficult decisions to make, with Ella having a couple of set backs post-surgery and being on more medicines than before surgery to now being on the fewest medicines ever. Noah had a rough fall last year also. He started off having a rough adjustment to his new class but has grown so much this year and is really excelling. I am so proud of both the kids. I am very happy to say that I have been able to really feel some peace over the last few months. 2012 is turning out to be a pretty good year. Don't get me wrong—the kids are still your typical kids and drive me crazy, but they are healthy and happy!*

*I suppose I am feeling pretty sappy today because Ella's kindergarten graduation was this morning. It was pretty sweet! The kids sang a few songs, said the Pledge of Allegiance, recited the school pledge, and counted to 100 by fives and tens. Then Mrs. Reed gave each child a folder with a few things the children had made and a picture of herself and Ella with a beautiful typed note. I did pretty well at the graduation until I read the note. Then the tears flowed. I started to read it in the parking lot, but when the tears came, I thought I had better read the rest at home because the people walking by would probably think I was nuts, thinking, "It's just kindergarten, lady. Get it together." If they only knew this is so much more than "just kindergarten." Oh my, so many tears I have shed over this little girl. If they were all contained, I bet I would have my own lake by now. With love, Angela*

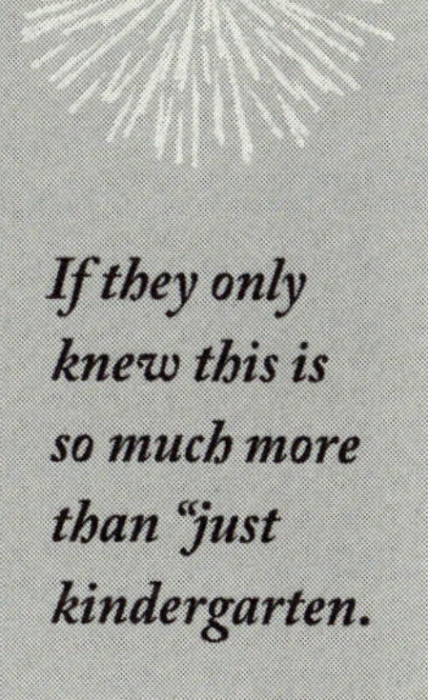


**The Lord listens.**

# Chapter 34

# GOD IS GOOD

*...all the time, and all the time, God is good.*

One of the most moving experiences I have had with Ella was about a year after her last surgery. I was discussing with Ella a book I had recently read. *Heaven is for Real* is about a young boy who, while in the hospital, experiences time in heaven. He told his mom and dad about who and what he saw while he was there. I told Ella that the little boy saw Jesus and was in heaven where the angels live. Her response stopped me in my tracks. She said, "Like the angels that were in my room?" I don't think my head could have turned to her any quicker. I asked, "What did you say?" She said that two angels were over her bed at the hospital. She further explained, "They had white dresses on, and I smiled at them."

I hugged her so tightly and told her, "I knew God was taking care of you." Although her experience was different than other children's, I have read of other children having heavenly visions. Joe was stunned by her words also. Our hearts grew a bit bigger, further knowing that He was comforting and protecting Ella all along. Not all stories end in miracles, but even in the heartache of losing loved ones, we can have comfort that God is in control, and we will see our loved ones again someday in the name of Jesus Christ.

As these last few years have passed by, Ella has continued to amaze us with her progress. She is now off ALL blood pressure and heart medicines—something her kidney doctor never thought possible and reminds us every time we see her. She always states that it really is a miracle how well Ella is doing. Ella will always be a Riley kid and have regular check-ups with nephrology and cardiology. We will forever be indebted to the doctors and nurses at Riley, family and friends, but most of all to our Lord for carrying us through this trial. As parents and with our earthly minds, we will always wonder how this will shape Ella as she becomes an adult. Will she embrace her differences and her scarred belly? We hope so. Or will it be an insecurity in this image exploited world? We certainly know that God didn't bring her through this for nothing, and we try to empower her everyday with the reminder that she is beautifully and uniquely made by God.

We have been blessed by people who have invited us to dance marathons and events to share our story as an encouragement to keep fundraising as it makes a difference in so many lives at the hospital. We try to find ways to give back to our community of family and friends who have given us so much that we can never repay. We are here to help each other. Be the community of brothers and sisters in Christ. Help those who can't help themselves. Pick people up when they have fallen.

It has taken me a few years to be obedient in putting our story into the words of this book. I'm not a "writer," but I do have a story. We ALL have a story. That January morning, God placed Big Daddy Weave's "My Story" song and video on the screen at church and placed in my heart that it was time to tell our story. I really wanted to fight it. Insecurities would flood my mind, and I would think, *Really, I'm not worthy of writing a book. People will critique me like crazy.* Thankfully, Joe and close friends spoke truth to me. Stories are meant to be shared, no matter how scary or muddy they may be. And through all this heartache and sweat and tears of writing out our story, if you are the one person who comes to Christ through reading it, then it was worth it, and this was for you because you are loved by our Heavenly Father. God bless you.

# Epilogue by Joe

Being a father can be tough, and being a father to a very young daughter going through some of the hardest moments of life can be heartbreaking. Then I see my wife fighting to meet the needs of our family and a young son who just wants her full attention and does what little boys do. When I start thinking back and remembering those times, so many emotions bubble to the surface. It can quickly overcome me if I stay in that moment too long.

When Angela shared with me how the Lord placed on her heart to write Ella's story, I selfishly wanted to keep it at arms-length for the reason I mentioned above. I don't know, maybe it's like a form of PTSD, reliving those memories of the unknown, medical decisions that were made without guarantees, feelings of failure and unworthiness, the eyes of my baby girl saying "HELP ME" as she was gasping for breath waking up with a breathing tube in her. I wasn't sure I could go back. It's challenging to describe what I feel inside.

I vividly remember when our loving Heavenly Father spoke truth to me through His Holy Spirit. He wanted me to know that the love HE has for Ella is far greater than mine. Although that seems impossible, it is true. He then allowed me to understand that He was in tears for what Ella was enduring. I would have never thought of that on my own. God was in control. That gave me the strength to move forward one day at a time.

I can also remember a time early in this journey when I was sharing with someone I worked with. After several minutes of sharing, he looked at me and said that Ella is truly a love story. It was days later when I realized what he really meant by saying that. He, too, was a Christ-follower. Those who have surrendered themselves and made Jesus the Savior of their lives by way of the cross know the greatest love story of all. This is Ella's love story—a message of hope and knowing the security of having Jesus as my Savior.

Ella is fifteen now, and she is growing into a loving young lady. She has many wonderful qualities, which she gets from Angela—even down to how she stands with her feet pointed the same way. It's funny. Ella was too young to remember a lot of what happened. Although we have shared those times with her, she doesn't have the same perspective as we do. That's okay. I am convinced that God will reveal His plan to her and allow her heart to know more of why it occurred. I call this the "lightbulb" moment, and I hope I am around when this happens.

I am very proud of my wife and her obedience. Angela and I will soon celebrate our twenty-fifth wedding anniversary. I know her better than anyone, and we are each other's person. She has reminded me that writing and sharing Ella's story is greater than the experience we went through. She is right.

Our prayer for Ella's story is that it's simply shared. God will do the rest.

# Note from Ella

Hello! My name is Ella, a fifteen-year-old girl whose life was changed forever at the age of just thirteen months. Although I don't remember much, a few things I do remember are that when it was time to take my medicine in the middle of the night, one of my nurses came and woke me up, and told me that it was time to take my medicine. She needed to go grab it. While she was gone, I looked at my mom to see if she was asleep, and she was totally knocked out in the chair next to me. I crawled out of my bed and snuck out of my room to go and hide from her, as a game, of course. When I walked out of my room, the first thing I saw was another one of my nurses sitting at her desk on her computer. I quickly rushed over there and asked her if I could hide under her desk. When I approached her, she looked a little puzzled as to why I was out of my room. With a chuckle, she allowed me to go under her desk. I waited for a few minutes, then a random fishing pole toy appeared in front of my face. I thought it was just my nurse whose desk I was under playing with me, but little did I know that it was my nurse who was going to give me my medicine trying to lure me out from under the desk. I fell for her trick and grabbed the toy, and she pulled me out for my medicine. Luckily, after the medicine, I was able to play under the desk a little while longer.

Another memory I have is when family and friends came to visit me in the hospital and gave me a bunch of get well and funny cards. One of the cards that I got was very funny. When I opened it, it would sing something a funny way. My mom has a video of it. As I kept opening it and sucking on a purple popsicle that I loved to get from the freezer near my room, I would sway my head back and forth with everyone laughing at my silliness. I also remember watching my favorite movie at the time, *Tangled*. I would watch that movie all the time. Good thing my mom liked that movie, too, or else I bet she would have gone crazy or ripped out her hair when I said I wanted to watch it for the four-millionth time.

I also remember when I walked to the playroom for the first time after one of my surgeries. It might not seem like that big of an accomplishment to some people, but for me, it felt like I had just hiked a five-mile trail. I remember while I was walking, I would have my arm wrapped around my stomach to help the pain. When I got to the playroom, I was so happy that I smiled so big. If I could have, I would have jumped with joy. I was definitely doing that on the inside, though.

I definitely have sad memories, too, but I don't know how to fully describe them. I will never forget my nurses and doctors. They have made a huge impact in my life. One of my favorite nurses came into my room and told me that she had a gift for me. She handed me a pair of starter earrings that were pink hearts that looked like crystals. I thanked her so much. When I got out of the hospital, I got my ears pierced, and I loved the earrings that she gave me. I feel like they matched my personality so well. All of my nurses were so nice and gentle, and I grew a huge connection to most of them. I love my doctors, too. These memories might not seem that important or special to some people, but these memories mean everything to me.

Now I am fifteen years old and healthy. No more medicine for me! To give back, every year we have a garage sale and whatever we raise goes toward Riley. The money we get is used to buy toys for the treasure chest at the blood draw center at Riley. The reason why we donate toys there is because, one year, my mom and I noticed that the treasure chest was empty. Having blood drawn can be scary, and I felt that the kids deserved to get a toy for being so brave. So, my mom and I decided to start buying toys with the money we get from our garage sales. I love giving back to the hospital that saved my life.

People say that God does things for a reason. I like to believe that what I went through is just the start of something huge that God is going to bring into my life, and I hope one day that God will give me the strength to take on whatever He has in store for me. I hope that for you, too.

# Timeline

**March 16, 1996** – Joe and Angela were married in their early twenties.

**July 1996** – Angela miscarried at twelve weeks.

**September 8, 2003** – Our sweet boy, Noah, was born.

**July 4, 2005** – Our little firecracker, Ella, was born.

**January 2006** – Ella had a great six-month checkup, and the nurse practitioner even said we could skip her nine-month checkup and she would see Ella back in July.

**May 2006** – We noticed that Ella had stopped growing and she was not hitting milestones, like crawling. Ella started seeing the doctor every two weeks for weight check and initial testing. We started keeping a food diary.

**July 4, 2006** – Ella turned one!

**July 31, 2006** – Ella seemed to have a cold, so I took her in to see the doctor. With a chest x-ray and an echocardiogram, she was found to be in heart failure and having dangerously high blood pressure. She was admitted to the Pediatric Intensive Care Unit at St. Vincent Hospital.

**August 4, 2006** – Ella was transferred to the Pediatric Intensive Care Unit at Riley Hospital for Children. They had a nephrologist on staff who could look into why Ella's blood pressure was so high.

**August 15, 2006** – Further testing found what was going on in Ella's body. We were given the diagnosis of abdominal aorta coarctation and stenosis in both renal arteries—narrowed areas that affected her blood flow to her kidneys and the lower half of her body. Her kidneys and heart were working overtime to make up for the loss of blood flow and that was wearing out her heart.

**August 19, 2006** – We were released from the hospital until doctors could design a plan.

**October 16, 2006** – Ella had major surgery by Dr. Brown and Dr. Rescorla to correct the narrowing areas in her body. This surgery truly saved her life and gave her the ability to thrive and grow.

**October 26, 2006** – Ella was able to go home.

**Spring of 2007** – We started attending Elston Family Church.

**May 2007** – Vomiting spells started. Ella would wake up in the early morning from a dead sleep and vomit ten to fourteen times in a matter of a few hours. Once it was over, she would act like nothing had happened.

**July 28, 2007** – We hosted a Celebration of Life party with our family and friends.

**January 2008** – Ella was diagnosed with cyclic vomiting syndrome by a gastrologist and medicine was added to the mix.

**February 2008** – Ella was admitted to the hospital for anemia. Hematology was now involved.

**Summer/Fall 2008** – Lots of doctor visits. Ella's blood pressure was gradually increasing.

**February 20, 2009** – A capsule endoscopy (pill cam) test found small bleeders in her upper intestines. This is what was causing her loss of blood and making her anemic, most likely a result of the major surgery. Medicine should help in healing the bleeders.

**March 19, 2009** – It had been found that as Ella grew, the narrowing in her right renal artery returned and was not growing with her. To help lower Ella's blood pressure, a balloon procedure was performed to open up the narrowed area.

**Fall/Winter 2009** – Still lots of doctor visits and tests. The vomiting spells had lessened and iron levels were looking good. Her blood pressure was increasing once again.

**July 1, 2010** – Second balloon procedure to open up that right renal artery and lower her blood pressure.

**Fall 2010** – Ella was growing and enjoying preschool. Noah was enjoying school as well. We believed the gastro issues had resolved.

**Spring 2011** – Ella's blood pressure was increasing again.

**June 2011** – The doctors could not continue to balloon open the narrowed area, so the transplant journey was underway.

**September 2011** – Angela was confirmed a kidney match with Ella, so in the case that the auto kidney transplant did not work, the doctor could transplant one of Angela's kidneys into Ella.

**October 10, 2011** – Auto kidney transplant surgery day. Dr. Goggins removed Ella's left, non-working kidney. He reconstructed the artery to her right kidney and transplanted her right kidney to a better blood flow area of her body. The surgery was a success!

**October 19, 2011** – Ella was released from hospital.

**October 21, 2011** – Ella had an overnight hospital stay when her levels were low.

**November 10, 2011** – Ella was back in the hospital for four days as her blood pressure was running really high and medicines were adjusted to bring it back into a safe range.

**May 2012** – Ella's blood pressure had stabilized in a great range, and Dr. Andreoli cut Ella's blood pressure medicines in half.

**June 20, 2012** – After six years of being on blood pressure medicines, Dr. Andreoli said we could take Ella off all blood pressure medicines, something she thought they would never be able to do. It continued to stay in a great range.

**October 2012** – Ella was granted a wish from the Make a Wish Foundation. We stayed at Give Kids the World, an amazing place.

**2013-2016** – Still regular visits (every four to six months) and blood pressure checks. She was doing great!

**2017-2020** – Moved to yearly cardiology appointments and six-month checkups with nephrology.

**July 4, 2020** – Ella turned fifteen. Ella will always be a Riley Kid and will always need to be monitored, but she is living her life.

# Letter from Aunt Stacie...
## Written in 2007

Dear Ella,

I thought that I better write something for your scrapbook since I didn't write any journal entries. The reason that there weren't any journal entries from me or Uncle Jim was because we were at the hospital with your mommy and daddy a lot.

You were at our house the day before you went into the hospital. Mommy was doing some Creative Memories stuff, and Daddy and Uncle Jim went golfing. You and Noah stayed at my house. It wasn't long ago, at your first birthday, that I told everyone that I was pregnant with your cousin Samantha. We were worried about you because you were not acting right—like you just weren't feeling well. I remember you sitting there, and then you would just fall over.

The next day, Mommy took you to the doctor and the next thing we knew, you were coming down to Indianapolis to St. Vincent Children's Hospital. We didn't hear anything, so went ahead and headed to the hospital. We found you still in the emergency room. They indicated that your heart was enlarged and initially indicated that a transplant could be possible. We were all just in shock. We stayed there and prayed with your mommy and daddy and the hospital chaplain. As we left the hospital and went home, we just cried and prayed for our precious little Ella.

Over the course of the next few weeks, we just prayed every day for you and wondered if this was going to be the day that the doctors would find out what was going on in your little body. Your mommy and daddy stayed by your side day and night. You are so lucky to have such great parents. Your mommy was so on top of everything. She would always ask all the right questions. When you finally got down to Riley Hospital, some of your toys were brought down. In addition to your blankie, your Baby Tad was a great comfort to you. I think that I sang "If You're Happy and You Know It" lots of times to you. I remember when Granny Walters came, and she and I stayed in the room with you while the others got dinner. She kept rubbing your foot, and you just loved it. If she would stop, then you would fuss. You also loved the "Head, Shoulders, Knees, and Toes" toy. We sang that song a lot, too.

We were so happy that your surgery was successful! I remember everyone crying tears of joy when we received the good news. It was amazing all the changes you went through from the start of your hospital stay until the day you were discharged. By the end, you were pulling up and standing in your crib bed!

You are a fighter, and I know that whatever challenges come your way in life, you will handle them with courage and bravery because you have already been through a lot, and you have a lot of people who love and support you.

Love you bunches,

Aunt Stacie, Uncle Jim, and Cousin Samantha

# Family Discussion Questions

Do you believe in miracles?

Do you believe miracles still occur today?

Do you see yourself in this story? If so, how?

What does this story teach or remind you about relationships? How can you apply these insights to yourself, a family member, or a friend?

Did the story move or confront you in some way? If so, which part? Did you notice anger, sadness, hope, or anything else arising in you? Did you sense yourself shutting down or opening up? Have you had a hurtful experience that requires more healing? If so, where, when, how, and with whom can you further your process?

_______________________________

_______________________________

_______________________________

_______________________________

_______________________________

_______________________________

_______________________________

Do you find yourself wanting a closer relationship with God? Do you believe that Jesus died on the cross for your sins? If so, you are welcomed to say the Salvation Prayer and read this out loud: *Heavenly Father, I have sinned, and I want your forgiveness for all my sins. I believe that Jesus died on the cross for me and rose again. Father, I give my life to you, and I want Jesus to come into my life and my heart. This I ask in Jesus' name. Amen!*

_______________________________

_______________________________

_______________________________

_______________________________

_______________________________

_______________________________

# About the McBrides

Joe and Angela met while in college at Indiana State University. They have been married now for twenty-four years. They are parents to Noah, Ella, and their black Lab, Chesney, and newly adopted Chihuahua mix, Panda.

Joe has worked in the insurance industry at State Farm Insurance for twenty-five years. He loves spending time with his family, camping, riding his motorcycle, and playing the game of golf. He enjoys traveling to the mountains and looks forward to spending more time out west.

Angela is a busy mom who is homeschooling Ella and enjoys volunteering with different organizations. She felt the tug on her heart a few years ago to share their story in book form in the hope that it would help another struggling family. She loves spending time with family and friends, traveling, playing games, and doing anything crafty.

Noah is seventeen and a junior in high school. He enjoys video games, golf, and working part-time at a locally-owned restaurant. He is looking forward to the day he can buy his dream car, a Nissan 370Z. He likes anything science-related and hopes to work in the field of science someday.

Ella is a freshman at the McBride Homeschooling Academy. She enjoys hanging out with her cousins and friends, babysitting, anything related to dogs and horses, and having her driver's permit. Someday she would love to own a horse. Her desire is to adopt children and show love to others as others have shown love to her.

As a family, the McBrides enjoy camping, traveling together, and going on new adventures.

Their hope in sharing their story is that you will find your own story within and you will see God's grace through it all.

For more information go to:

facebook.com/EllasStoryBook2020

www.EllasStoryBook2020.com

Or contact at:

angmcbride225@gmail.com

Made in the USA
Middletown, DE
07 November 2021